1950's BOXING
IN BLACK & WHITE

By
Larry Carli

1950's Boxing in Black and White

ISBN: 978-1-61170-308-5

Front Cover Photo: Rocky Marciano vs. Roland LaStarza 1953 *www.wbaboxing.com.*

Back Cover Photo: Ray Robinson. *International Boxing,* February, 1973

Published by:

Rp **Robertson Publishing**™
www.RobertsonPublishing.com

Printed in the USA and UK on acid-free paper.

To purchase additional prints of this book go to:
amazon.com
barnesandnoble.com

Larry Carli has also written:
- *Boxing's Super 70's*
- *The Top Ten Middleweight Champions of All Time: Who Was The Greatest?*

Foreword

The 1950's has been called the age of simplicity by various authors over the years. In the 1940's the United States was involved in World War 2, and the 1960's was a violent time of cultural changes, as the nation saw massive demonstrations against the Vietnam War, assassinations of political leaders such as President John F. Kennedy, his brother Robert F. Kennedy, and Civil Rights leader Martin Luther King Junior.

Sandwiched between these two violent decades was the 1950's a time of relative calm and prosperity in American culture. The 1950's was a decade of peaceful serenity, and a time when Americans sat in their living rooms and watched boxing 3 nights a week on their black and white box shaped television sets cheering on their favorite fighters.

Table of Contents

Table of Contents (cont.)

Rocky Marciano
Photograph from The Ring, February,1956

CHAPTER 1   HEAVYWEIGHTS

ROCKY MARCIANO

Rocco Francis Marchegiano was born to Pierno and Pasqualena in Brockton, Massachusetts on September 1, 1923. He was the firstborn son of Pierino and Pasqualena Marchegiano. Rocco grew up watching his father work for low wages and long hours in the Brockton shoe factories. The fear of poverty remained with him for his whole life and helped him to succeed in everything that he tried in his life.

After completing high school, Rocco joined the Army and served in Wales and Ft. Lewis, Washington. When he got out he tried out for a Chicago Cubs farm team. Rocco failed to make the team due to his inability to throw from home to second base in a crouch and decided to try his hand at boxing. As it was, Rocky had boxed in a few matches in the Army to avoid kitchen duty, and he flashed some punching power in his novice amateur matches.

Rocky was in desperate need of some money, and he turned professional in March of 1947 by knocking out Lee Epperson in 3 rounds. In 1948 Rocco obtained the services of well-known fight manager Al Weill and trainer Charley Goldman who trained five world champions in his career. One of the first things Weill did was to change Rocco's ring name to Rocky Marciano, as the fight announcers had a hard time pronouncing his legal name of Rocco Marchegiano.

1

Under the guidance of trainer Charley Goldman, and fighting mainly out of Providence, Rhode Island in small fight clubs, Rocky went undefeated in 1948 by winning all 11 of his fights by knockout. Rocky's powerful right hand made up for his crudeness in the ring in the early part of his career.

After 16 straight knockouts Rocky had to go the distance for the first time when he won a 10-round decision over the defensively minded Don Mogard in May of 1948 in Providence. Rocky showed incredible stamina during the fight as he was throwing bombs at Mogard for the whole 10-round fight.

Rocky returned to the ring with 3 quick knockouts, but he again had to go the 10-round distance when he took a unanimous decision over Tiger Ted Lowry in October of 1949. Lowry was very tall, awkward, and was already a veteran of over 70 professional fights. Rocky won the fight, but Lowry made him look bad with his defensive style. Some of the ringside reporters gave Lowry as many as 4 rounds, but there was no doubt that Rocky really won the fight. Rocky would later say, when his ring career was over, that Lowry had the style to go the distance with him in 10 out of 10 fights.

On December 19th in 1949 Rocky looked good in stopping veteran heavyweight Phil Muscato in 5 rounds in Providence. Goldman advised Al Weill that he thought Rocky was ready to fight in New York after the Muscato fight. Weill, who actually doubled as Rocky's manager and a matchmaker for Madison Square Garden, booked Rocky for a 10-round main event against the hard punching veteran Carmine Vingo on December 30th.

The Vingo fight was an absolute war. The two Italian-American bulls took turns staggering each other during the early rounds and Vingo hitting the deck twice. Every time Vingo looked like he was ready to be knocked out, he would roar back and stagger Rocky with right hands.

Rocky finally broke through in the 6th round when he clipped Vingo with a short left hook which dropped him to the canvas. Vingo hit the back of his head hard on the canvas when he went down and was counted out by the referee.

While Rocky was celebrating his victory in the ring, it became apparent that Vingo was in severe distress while lying on the canvas and had to be transported to the hospital where he lapsed into a coma. Vingo eventually came out of the coma in the hospital, but his ring career was over as Rocky's career was just beginning. Though his own career was over, Vingo became one of Rocky's biggest fans and followed his former opponent's ring career closely.

Rocky's next opponent would be top New York heavyweight prospect Roland LaStarza. LaStarza was a good looking, young, undefeated fighter with 37 wins to his credit. LaStarza's good looks brought women to his fights, and he had a smooth counter punching style of fighting that brought in the men in the crowd. Though LaStarza lacked real power he made up for it with finesse and charisma to become a big gate attraction. The fight was finally set for March of 1950, and LaStarza's manager Jimmy "Fats" DeAngelo felt that his fighter had the style to defeat the strong but crude style of fighting that Rocky brought into the ring with him.

Rocky appeared nervous when he entered the ring. LaStarza wasted no time as he took the first 3 rounds by counterpunching and evading Rocky's wild right hand swings. Finally, in the 4th round Rocky broke through LaStarza's defense and dropped him hard to the canvas with a right hand. LaStarza survived the round and stayed away from Rocky in the 5th round. Rocky lost one of the middle rounds for a low-blow, and he had to come on strong towards the end of the fight to make it close. Rocky fought hard and aggressively in the 9th and 10th rounds, but LaStarza matched him punch for punch. The fight was very close and no one in the Garden was absolutely sure who had won.

One judge voted for LaStarza and one judge voted for Rocky. The referee Jack Watson gave 5 rounds to each fighter; but he gave the fight to Rocky on points for his aggressiveness. This would be the closest Rocky ever came to losing a professional fight. The loss was heartbreaking for LaStarza as it would take him 3 more years before he could get Rocky in the ring with him for a world title fight. DeAngelo, LaStarza's manager, was so mad after the fight that he slammed the door in Al Weill's face when he went to congratulate LaStarza on a great fight. This insult would come back to hurt LaStarza's chances of getting an immediate return match with Rocky and ended up costing him three valuable years of his fighter's career.

Rocky continued his winning ways and cracked the top 10 heavyweight rankings after the LaStarza fight. In July of 1951 Rocky chopped down Utah strongboy Rex Layne in 6 rounds to set up a big money fight with ex-champion Joe Louis. Rocky stepped into the ring to face Louis in October of 1951. Louis was past his prime, but he was still a dangerous opponent for an up-and-coming heavyweight like Rocky. Louis puffed up Rocky's face with stinging jabs, but he was trapped on the ropes and knocked out of the ring by Rocky for an 8th round technical knockout. It was a sad sight to see the once great Joe Louis sprawled out on the ring apron after the knockout

In July of 1952 Rocky was matched with the beefed-up light heavyweight contender Harry Matthews in an elimination match to determine champion Jersey Joe Walcott's next opponent. Matthews had been promised a shot at the light heavyweight champion Joey Maxim's title, but manager Jack Hurley instead opted to face Rocky in hopes of getting a future shot at the heavyweight championship.

Matthews came out in the first round and outboxed Rocky rather easily. In the 2nd round Rocky trapped Matthews in a corner and knocked him out with two rapid fire left hooks to the head. Rocky was just too strong for the 180-pound Matthews. Rocky was now the number one contender to Walcott's heavyweight championship. The heavyweight title fight was set for September of 1952 in Philadelphia.

Rocky got off to a poor start in his title fight as he was decked for the first time in his career in the 1st round by a Walcott left hook. Rocky got up, more embarrassed than hurt, at the count of 3. Rocky finished the first round with a swollen left eye. Walcott was fighting one of his best fights in years as his punches were cutting Rocky and he had him blinking his eyes throughout the middle rounds. Rocky would later claim that he was blinded by some type of liniment that he felt was on Walcott's gloves. Rocky fought back hard, but at the end of 12 rounds he was behind in the scoring and it looked like he needed a knockout to win the title.

In the 13th round, Rocky followed Walcott to the ropes, and fired a short right hand to the head and grazed his head as he was going down with a left hook. Walcott lay, sprawled, on the canvas and did not move a muscle as he was counted out. Rocky was the new Heavyweight Boxing Champion of the world. It was a fight for the ages and is still talked about to this day. Rocky's incredible stamina and punching power were just too much for the aging Walcott to overcome at a late point in the fight.

After winning the title everybody, multimillionaires, athletes, and celebrities, wanted to be around the champ. However, Al Weill was an astute businessman, and his first order of business was to get Rocky back into the ring for a rematch with Walcott. The rematch was set for May of 1953 in Chicago.

Rocky tagged Walcott in the very first round with a right uppercut at close quarters which most fight fans did not see. Walcott fell backward with his feet high in the air. Walcott failed to beat the 10 count and jumped up ready to fight as soon as he was counted out. Ringsiders booed lustily and Walcott would later claim that he "blacked out" during the middle of the count and did not hear it.

Walcott retired immediately after the fight, and the fight itself did nothing to enhance Rocky's reputation.

Rocky's next opponent was Roland LaStarza. Since his 1950 defeat to Rocky, LaStarza had won 15 of 17 fights while avoiding other top contenders like Ezzard Charles, and Nino Valdes. LaStarza won a title eliminator match against Rex Layne in February of 1953 and Rocky wanted to set the record straight as to who was the better fighter after his 1950 close call with LaStarza. Rocky's fight with LaStarza was set for September of 1953 in New York.

Rocky came out cautiously in the early rounds and, for some reason, he seemed like he wanted to box LaStarza. LaStarza won the early rounds by moving and counterpunching. At the end of 6 rounds LaStarza was ahead in the scoring and Rocky appeared listless and had a round taken away due to a low blow.

After the 6th round, Rocky's corner told him he was losing the fight and would have to increase the pace of the fight. Rocky came out swinging in the 7th round, and battered LaStarza all over the ring by banging into his head, midsection, and arms. By the end of the round LaStarza was suffering broken blood vessels in his arms and took a frightful beating the rest of the way. In the 11th round Rocky knocked LaStarza through the ropes and down onto the ring apron. LaStarza was game and he got up before the 10 count. Rocky was battering him at will when the referee stepped between them and stopped the fight and gave Rocky an 11th round technical knockout victory. LaStarza said after the fight that Rocky was "five thousand times tougher" than he was in their first fight. LaStarza was never the same after his title fight, and he retired in 1955 after losing more fights than he had won after his title defeat at the hands of Rocky.

Rocky did not fight again until May of 1954 when he defended against the former heavyweight champion and top contender Ezzard Charles. This fight would prove to be Rocky's toughest title defense.

The fight was held in Madison Square Garden, New York. Charles came out fast and looked like the Charles of old as he was boxing and moving out of the reach of Rocky's wild counter punches. Charles had a sting in his punches and he was starting to cut Rocky's face up.

By the 5th round Rocky settled down, and his strong body punching was starting to slow Charles down. Charles fought back hard, but it was difficult to keep Rocky off of him. By the 10th round, Rocky had caught up with Charles in the scoring, and he had damaged Charles' Adam's apple with a punch to the throat.

Rocky continued to give Charles a terrible beating from the 11th round on, but Charles came back and won the 14th round in a last gasp effort to take the title. Rocky came back in the 15th and final round and battered a game Charles all over the ring. Charles would be the only title challenger in Rocky's career to finish the fight on his feet.

The decision was unanimous in Rocky's favor, but Charles certainly deserved a rematch due to his game effort. Charles gained more stature with his strong challenge for the title, than he did for his two-year title reign as champion from 1949 to 1951.

James D. Norris and the International Boxing Club set the rematch for September of 1954 again in Madison Square Garden. Rocky came out aggressively at the start of the fight and wasted no time in dropping Charles to the canvas in the 2nd round. It appeared that Rocky wanted to get the fight over with quickly and not engage in a 15-round war.

Rocky took complete control of the fight and battered Charles from the 3rd through the 5th rounds. Charles came out aggressively in the 6th round realizing that this was probably his last chance to regain his title. Rocky came out of a clinch near the end of the round with blood streaming down his face from a cut nostril. Rocky returned to his corner and it was discovered that his nostril was actually sliced in half and they could not stop the bleeding. Rocky came out aggressively for the 7th round, and he chased Charles all over the ring trying for the knockout. Charles fought back and made it to the end of the round.

Rocky came back to his corner, and he was advised that if he did not knock Charles out in the 8th round that the fight would probably be stopped because they could not stop the bleeding coming from his sliced nose. Rocky came storming out for the 8th round and he immediately dropped Charles to the canvas. Charles got up, but Rocky was all over him and dropped him to the canvas for the second time. Charles popped up immediately after the 10 count was completed and Rocky held on to his title just when it seemed like the fight was ready to be stopped because of his cut nose.

It took a long time for Rocky's cut nose to heal and he was starting to lose his desire to fight. Rocky was spending a lot of time away from his family, and he really disliked Al Weill's dictatorial style of managing. Weill eventually convinced Rocky to get back into the ring in May of 1955 against lightly regarded British heavyweight Don Cockell. The fight was to be in San Francisco, California, in hopes of bringing out a lot of Rocky's Italian fans from the surrounding area to see the fight. The fight would be held at the Cow Palace in Daly City, a suburb of San Francisco. Cockell had a roly poly physique and was really just a blown-up light heavyweight. Cockell really did not have a heavyweight punch, but he could box, and he was known to be durable.

Rocky battered Cockell all over the ring from the first round on. Cockell could take a great deal of punishment, but he did not have the power to hurt Rocky or keep away from him in the ring. Rocky fought a rough, tough, foul-filled fight and missed a lot of his punches. At one point he actually struck Cockell while he was down near the ropes, but the referee did not call a foul and Cockell made it to his feet. The referee had seen enough by the 9th round as Cockell had just become a punching bag. Rocky was given the 9th round technical knockout win for one of his sloppier title defenses.

Rocky wanted one more big payday before he retired and he found the ideal opponent in light heavyweight champion Archie Moore. Moore was thought to be around 40 years old, and he had been the light heavyweight champion since 1952. He was called the Old Mongoose as he could punch and had loads of charisma. Moore went public about wanting a title shot against Marciano, and he had won a title elimination match against the big Cuban Nino Valdes to qualify for the title challenge. Moore claimed that Marciano was clumsy and that he could not really hit him due to his excellent defensive skills. Moore was an artist when it came to building up the gate for a fight. The fight was eventually set for September of 1955 in Yankee Stadium.

Moore came out fast in the first round of the title fight and immediately dropped Rocky to his knee with a left hook as he was coming into close quarters. Rocky's right knee and gloves touched the canvas, and he was up at the count of 2 — more embarrassed than hurt — when he popped up from the canvas. Referee Harry Kessler forgot that the mandatory 8 count had been waived for the fight and started the count. When Kessler got to around the count of about 5 he realized his mistake and he ordered the fighters together to continue the match. Moore always felt that Kessler's mistake gave Rocky precious seconds to recover and that the mistake probably cost him the fight. In all honesty it appeared that Rocky's title was not saved by the referee.

Moore put up a spirited battle and avoided many of Rocky's punches, but Rocky just kept throwing non-stop shots and he finally dropped Moore to the canvas in the 6th round. Moore got up and fought back until he was dropped again in the 8th round. The referee went to Moore's corner at the end of the 8th round and he was asked if he wished to continue to fight. Moore advised the referee that he was also a champion, and that he would rather be counted out in the ring than lose the fight sitting on his stool in the corner.

Moore came out for the 9th round and attacked, but Rocky drove him into a corner and dropped him. Moore was too exhausted and beat to get up before the 10 count as he was in a seated position with his arms hanging over the side of the ropes. This would be the final fight of Rocky's career and the 6th defense of his title.

In May of 1956, claiming a back injury and wanting to spend more time with his family, Rocky retired from the ring in a press conference held in New York. In all reality Rocky was sick of the training grind, and he felt that his manager, Al Weill, had held out money from some of his purses.

The heavyweight champion in the 1950s was looked upon with great respect. There was only one heavyweight champion at the time, and different organizations like the World Boxing Organization, International Boxing Federation, and the World Boxing Council were not in existence in the 1950's. Because he had managed to retire with a perfect ring record of 49 wins and no loses Rocky was considered thee heavyweight champion of the 1950's.

Upon his retirement in 1956, Rocky, along with Jack Johnson and Jack Dempsey, were considered by many to be the greatest heavyweight champions in history. After his retirement Rocky never returned to the ring, though he did flirt with the idea of making a comeback in 1959 when Ingemar Johansson was champion.

Rocky was one of the original members inducted into the International Boxing Hall of Fame in 1990. Sadly Rocky perished in an airplane crash one day before his 46th birthday in 1969. Rocky's final ring record was 49 wins with no losses or draws. He won 43 fights by knockout.

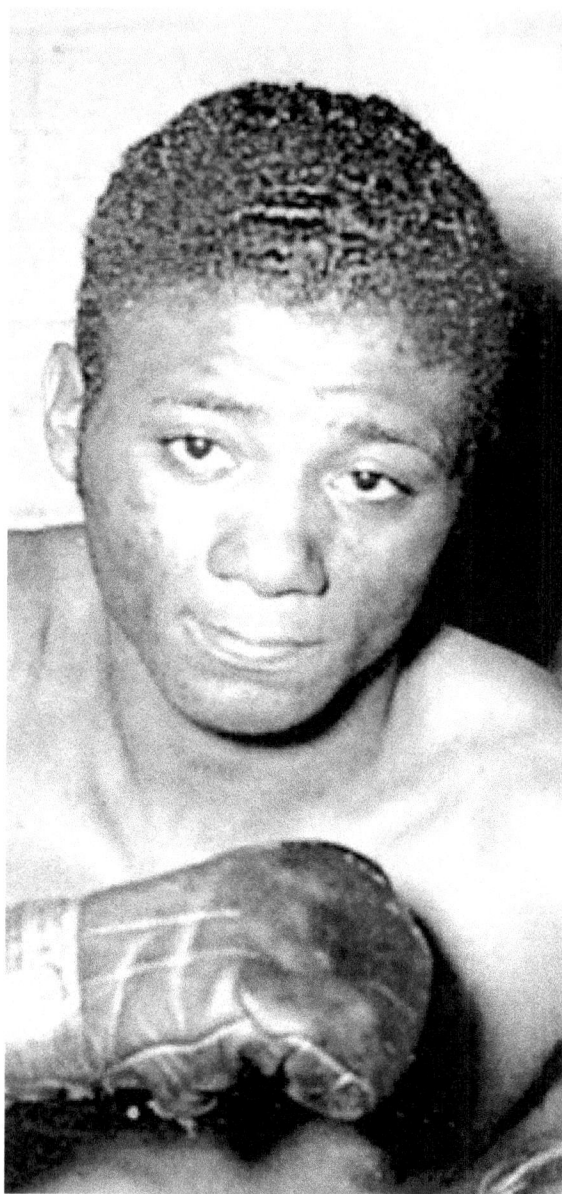

Floyd Patterson
Television Boxing Guide, 1954

FLOYD PATTERSON

Floyd Patterson was the youngest man in the history of the heavyweight division at the time to win the title in November of 1956 at just 21 years of age. Floyd was also the first man in the heavyweight division to regain the title when he knocked out Ingemar Johansson in 1960.

Floyd's reputation suffered from the fact that he followed the legend of Rocky Marciano as heavyweight champion of the world. Ezzard Charles suffered a similar fate when he followed Joe Louis as heavyweight champion.

Floyd was born in Waco, North Carolina on January 4, 1935. He was one of eleven children in a poor family. His family moved to New York when he was 10 years old. Floyd had a troubled childhood and spent several years in reform schools for truancy and a wide variety of thefts. He later credited them with turning his life around.

Floyd took up amateur boxing at the age of 14 and, fighting out of the Gramercy gym, became the National Amateur Middleweight champion. Three years later Floyd qualified for the United States Olympic boxing team and caught the eye of New York boxing promoter Cus D'Amato. Floyd then traveled to Helsinki, Finland in 1952 and won the gold medal in the middleweight division. In winning the gold medal Floyd exhibited "fast hands" and knockout power with both fists.

Cus D'Amato helped Floyd develop a "peek a boo" type of defense in which he carried his hands high in front of his face. Under

13

D'Amato's guidance Floyd also developed a very powerful left hook.

Floyd turned professional as a light heavyweight under D'Amato's guidance and won his first 13 professional fights. Floyd suffered his first loss as a professional when former light heavyweight champion Joey Maxim won a close and controversial 8-round decision over him in June of 1954. Most of the ringside boxing observers felt that Floyd won the fight, but the judges voted unanimously for Maxim.

In 1955 Floyd moved up to the heavyweight division and went on a 16-bout winning streak, and then found himself matched with the top contender Tommy "Hurricane" Jackson in an elimination match to face Archie Moore for Rocky Marciano's vacated heavyweight title.

Floyd took on Jackson in June of 1956 in New York. Floyd did not look exceptionally good in the fight and appeared vulnerable as he won a close 12-round decision over the flashy Jackson. The judges preferred Floyd's steady boxing over Jackson's flashy eye-catching flurries. The stage was now set for Floyd to challenge Moore later in the year for the heavyweight title.

Moore was the sentimental favorite among fans in the fight for Rocky Marciano's vacated title, and boxing's wise guys felt that he was too experienced for Floyd based on his determined effort in the Marciano fight the year before. The fight was set for Chicago in November of 1956.

Floyd proved too fast for Moore and he made him look like an old man in the ring. Youth was definitely served as Floyd punched his way to an easy 5th round technical knockout. Moore could not get out of the way of Floyd's left hooks and a perfect hard hook to the jaw finished off the Old Mongoose in the 5th round. Many fight fans were surprised by Floyd's hand speed and how bad he made Moore look in the fight.

Floyd became the youngest fighter to ever win the heavyweight title, and he also became a father for the first time as his wife delivered a baby girl earlier in the day. Floyd was not told of his first child until his fight with Moore was over out of fear that he would not enter the ring out of a preference to be with his wife and daughter. After all the victory celebrations, Floyd started preparing for his first title defense: a rematch with top contender Tommy "Hurricane" Jackson. The first fight with Jackson was a disputed decision win, and Floyd wanted to prove his superiority over Jackson. The rematch with Jackson was set for July of 1957 in New York.

Floyd came out with fire in his heart at the start of the fight and dropped Jackson in the first and second rounds. He did not want any controversy to surround this fight. Jackson came out flashing his combinations and playing to the crowd in the middle rounds, but Floyd was the stronger puncher, and he dropped Jackson again in the 9th round. There would be no letup in Floyd's attack on this night, and he began to pummel Jackson with hardly a return until the referee showed mercy and stopped the fight in the 10th round to save Jackson from further punishment. There was no doubt about it: by 1957 the public knew that Floyd was the best heavyweight in the world.

Floyd's next opponent would be the 1956 Olympic boxing heavyweight champion Pete Rademacher. Rademacher had never fought as a professional and his promotional group was offering D"Amato a quarter of a million dollars for the fight to be held in Rademacher's hometown of Seattle, Washington. D'Amato jumped at the chance for the money and somehow was able to have the match sanctioned for the heavyweight championship. The fight was to be held in August in Rademacher's hometown.

Rademacher rushed out at the opening bell and went right after Floyd, dropping him to the canvas in the second round. Floyd withstood the attack and eventually wore down the Olympian for a 7th round technical knockout. Floyd collected the money, but the fight went a long way toward damaging his reputation, as an amateur making his professional debut dropped him to the canvas.

In 1958 D'Amato again sidestepped the top contenders Eddie Machen and Zora Folley, and signed Floyd to defend his title against an unbeaten but also unknown heavyweight contender named Roy Harris from the hamlet of Cut N Shoot, Texas. The fight was held in August of 1958 in Los Angeles, California.

Harris dropped Floyd to the canvas early in the fight, but he was eventually worn down and stopped by the relentlessness of Floyd in the 12th round. Though he was victorious, Floyd was developing the reputation of having a "glass jaw" as he had been dropped by two straight contenders who were not thought to be heavy punchers. While Floyd was defending his title against second rate opponents, Sweden's Ingemar Johansson surprised everyone by knocking out top contender Eddie Machen in one round in Sweden. Machen's knockout allowed Floyd the opportunity to squeeze in another easy title defense before taking on the big Swede. In May of 1959 Floyd defended his title against British punching bag Brian London. Floyd knocked London out in the 11th round of a gross mismatch — with the only surprise being that Floyd was not dropped in the fight. The stage was now set for Floyd to defend against the new number one contender: Johansson.

The Swedish challenger was largely unknown in the United States, other than the fact that he had knocked Eddie Machen cold in the 1st round earlier in the year. Johansson arrived in the United States with his girlfriend Birgit Lungren, and he exhibited odd training habits with the press maintaining that he was out of shape for the fight. The fight was set for June of 1959 in New York's Yankee Stadium.

After two boring rounds, the 3rd round brought excitement as Johansson who had just been flicking out a left jab suddenly struck with his big right hand that he nicknamed "toonder" and Floyd was on the canvas in another title defense. Johansson did not let Floyd off the hook as he dropped him a total of 7 times before the referee saved Floyd from more punishment and declared Johansson the new heavyweight champion.

The press labeled Floyd a "cheese" champion and claimed that the first top contender that he had faced since Tommy Jackson had knocked him flat on his face. Floyd felt the humiliation and went into hibernation to prepare for the Johansson rematch in June of 1960 in Yankee Stadium.

Floyd was a completely different fighter in the rematch. After being stung by a Johansson right hand high on his forehead in the 2nd round Floyd concentrated his attack on Johansson's midsection. Floyd went for the knockout in the 5th round, and he got it by knocking Johansson out cold with a leaping left hook that left Johansson lying on the canvas with his eyes glazed, one leg twitching, and blood pouring out the side of his mouth. Floyd became the first heavyweight champion in history to regain the heavyweight championship. Floyd's victory set the stage for the rubber match to be held in Miami Beach in March of 1961. Johansson trained poorly for the rubber match and it was evident when he entered the ring for battle.

Johansson caught Floyd coming in and drew first blood with a knockdown early in the fight. Johansson was then caught and dropped by Floyd's left hook as he left himself wide open while going for the knockout. Johansson's poor physical condition finally caught up to him and he was dropped and stopped by Floyd in the 6th round. This fight ended the trilogy of their rivalry and the two became lifelong friends after their careers were over with.

With victories over Eddie Machen and Zora Folley, ex-convict Sonny Liston became the number one contender for Floyds crown by the end of 1961. D'Amato hoped to avoid Liston and took an easy title defense against Tom McNeely in Toronto, Canada in December of 1961.

Floyd dropped McNeely about 10 times during the fight and stopped him in the 4th round of the mismatch. Floyd, as was customary, was also dropped to one knee by a McNeely right hand to the temple during the fight. Despite D'Amato's objections, Floyd signed to fight top contender Sonny Liston in September of 1962 in Chicago.

Floyd came out in the first round and looked very tentative as he went down from the first real punches that Liston threw. Floyd did not get up before the 10 count and he lost his title in a totally non-competitive title fight. Floyd donned a disguise and slipped away from the post-fight crowd and went into hiding. Floyd kept a low profile until his rematch with Liston in July of 1963 in Las Vegas.

At the sound of the first bell, Liston came out looking for the knockout and, before anyone knew it, Floyd was on the canvas. He lasted 4 seconds longer in the rematch than when he lost his title to Liston in 1962. Liston was just too big and strong for weak-chinned Floyd. This fight marked the end of Floyd's championship days.

Floyd would continue fighting and beat top contenders Eddie Machen and George Chuvalo to set up a title challenge against champion Muhammed Ali in 1965. Ali labeled Floyd "the rabbit" for the title fight that was held in November in Las Vegas.

Public sympathy was for Floyd in this fight, but Ali was too big and fast for Floyd. To make matters worse, Floyd injured his back during the fight and the mismatch was eventually stopped in the 12th round when Floyd was unable to continue.

Floyd returned to the ring in 1966 and knocked out British champion Henry Cooper in 4 rounds. In 1967 Floyd was entered into a heavyweight tournament to determine the successor to Muhammed Ali who had been stripped of his title for refusing military induction. Floyd was eliminated in the quarterfinals of the tournament when he lost a disputed majority decision to contender Jerry Quarry.

In September of 1968, Floyd challenged the World Boxing Association champion Jimmy Ellis for the title in Stockholm, Sweden. Ellis was given the 15-round decision by the referee despite the crowd's overwhelming negative reaction to the verdict. This would be the last title fight that Floyd would participate in.

In February of 1972, Floyd would decision the top ten heavyweight contender Oscar Bonavena to set up a rematch with Muhammed Ali. The rematch with Ali was held in September of 1972 in New York. In the last fight of his career Floyd was dominated and stopped by cuts in the 7th round. Floyd never actually announced his retirement; he just never fought again.

In retirement Floyd became head of the New York State athletic commission and was elected into the International Boxing Hall of Fame in 1991. Floyd passed away in 2006 at the age of 71. Floyd's final ring record was 55 wins, 8 loses, and 1 draw. He won 40 fights by knockout.

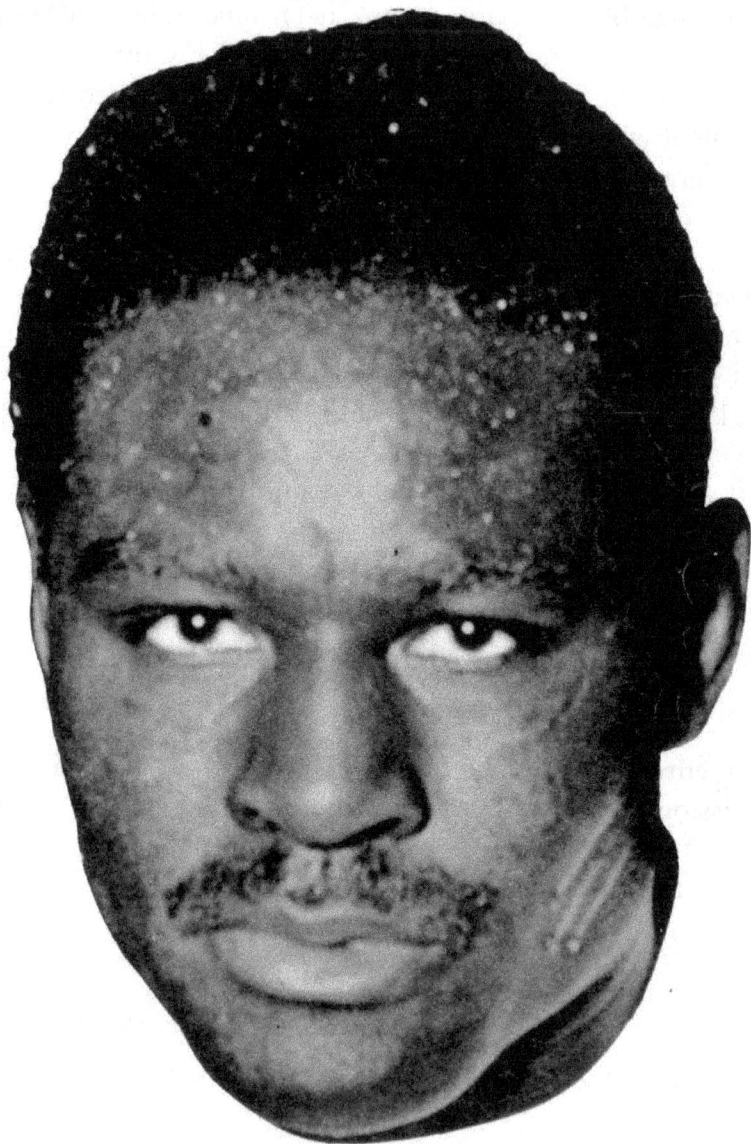

Ezzard Charles
Boxing Illustrated February 1971

EZZARD CHARLES

Ezzard Mack Charles was born in Lawrenceville, Georgia on July 21, 1921. Charles' family settled in Cincinnati, Ohio where he quickly became an amateur boxing star. Ezzard won the Diamond belt middleweight championship, Chicago Golden Gloves, and Amateur Athletic Union middleweight championships in 1939.

After compiling a perfect 42 win and 0 loss amateur boxing record, Ezzard turned professional in 1940 under the managerial reins of Jack Mintz, and Tom Tannas. Ezzard won his first 17 professional fights as a middleweight before losing a 10-round decision to the clever former middleweight champion Ken Overlin in June of 1941 in Cincinnati, Ohio.

Ezzard fought sporadically during the war years as he grew into a light heavyweight. Ezzard defeated former middleweight champion Teddy Yarosz in November of 1941 and former light heavyweight champion Anton DeCristofordis in January of 1942. Ezzard defeated the great Charley Burley twice by decision in 1942 and held Ken Overlin to a draw in a rematch. Ezzard closed out the year by also defeating future light heavyweight champion Joey Maxim twice by decision.

Ezzard lost a couple of matches in Cleveland in 1943, and then went into the United States Army during war time where he boxed in Inter-Allied tournaments in Italy and North Africa.

Ezzard won all 10 of his matches in 1946 after returning from the war. He obtained a top 10 light heavyweight ranking when he defeated the likes of Archie Moore, Lloyd Marshall, and Jimmy Bivins.

Ezzard defeated Moore, Marshall, and Bivins in rematches in 1947 while waiting for a title shot at Gus Lesnevich's light heavyweight title. In January of 1948 Ezzard knocked out Archie Moore for his 3rd straight victory over the future light heavyweight champion, and then took on young light heavyweight Sam Baroudi in Chicago in February. Ezzard gave Baroudi a fearful beating before stopping him in 10 rounds. Baroudi died from the injuries he suffered in the fight, and Ezzard seemed to have lost his "killer instinct" after Baroudi's death.

Unable to get a title fight with light heavyweight champion Gus Lesnevich, Ezzard moved up to the heavyweight division to defeat Jimmy Bivins and Joey Maxim in rematches as part of a heavyweight elimination tournament. In June of 1949 Ezzard was matched with Jersey Joe Walcott for the vacant National Boxing Association heavyweight title. The title had been vacated by Joe Louis when he announced his retirement. The match was set for June of 1949 in Chicago.

Ezzard won a unanimous decision over Walcott in a flawless but methodical performance. Ezzard deserved the decision, but it was a somewhat boring fight between two counter punchers which did not excite the fans. Due to this lack of flash, Ezzard's title was not recognized in New York and in other parts of the world.

In August of 1949 Ezzard defended his National Boxing Association heavyweight title against former light heavyweight champion Gus Lesnevich in New York. Ezzard gave Lesnevich a severe beating and stopped him in the 7th round. Some ring observers felt that Ezzard was exacting revenge on Lesnevich for denying him a shot at the light heavyweight title earlier in the decade.

Ezzard was a fighting champion and in October of 1949 he traveled to San Francisco, California to stop local Italian favorite Pat Valentino in 8 rounds. Further, in August of 1950 Ezzard traveled to Buffalo, New York to battle veteran competitor Freddy Beshore. Beshore came to fight, but Ezzard eventually wore him down and stopped him in the 14th round of the title fight. Arrangements were then made for Ezzard to fight the comebacking Joe Louis for worldwide heavyweight title recognition in September in New York.

Ezzard gave Louis a severe beating for 15 rounds and appeared to ease up on him in the late rounds as he did not appear to go for the knockout victory. Louis was obviously past his prime, and he never seriously challenged the champion during the 15-round distance. Ezzard was given the unanimous decision and, with the victory, he gained worldwide recognition as heavyweight champion of the world.

In December of 1950 Ezzard returned home to Cincinnati to stop the veteran contender Nick Barone in 11 rounds. In January of 1951 Ezzard was back in the ring defending his title against heavyweight contender Lee Oma. Oma came to fight and put up a decent struggle against Ezzard until he was stopped in the 10th round of the title fight.

In March of 1951 Ezzard gave Joe Walcott a rematch for the title in Detroit, Michigan. Ezzard dropped Walcott in the rematch, and he won another unanimous decision over the veteran contender.

In May of 1951 Ezzard defended his title for the 8th time against light heavyweight champion Joey Maxim in Chicago. Ezzard was too strong for Maxim and won an easy decision over the Cleveland native.

In July of 1951 Ezzard traveled to Pittsburgh to defend his title against perennial contender Joe Walcott. This was the 3rd meeting between the two fighters, but it is unclear why this fight was made as their two previous meetings were not box office successes.

In a major upset during the 7th round, Walcott uncorked a left hook to the jaw to knock Ezzard out and separate him from his crown. Their 3rd fight was a charm for Walcott as he finally grabbed the world heavyweight title in his 5th overall try for the belt.

Ezzard returned to the ring in October and stopped Rex Layne in 11 rounds in Pittsburgh. Ezzard finished out the year by defeating Joey Maxim again, and Joe Kahut to qualify for another heavyweight title fight with Joe Walcott in June of 1952. Walcott defended against Ezzard in Philadelphia for their 4th meeting.

Walcott was given the 15-round decision in a drab and boring fight. Neither fighter showed much fire during the fight, and the decision could have gone either way. Ezzard never really did enough during the fight to take the title and the sentimental decision went to Walcott.

In August of 1952 Ezzard lost a decision in a rematch with Rex Layne, but defeated contenders Cesar Brion, and Jimmy Bivins to close out the year. In April of 1953 Ezzard won a decision over Rex Layne in a rubber match, but then lost decisions to Nino Valdes, and Harold Johnson. Ezzard closed out the year by knocking out Coley Wallace in San Francisco.

In January of 1954 Ezzard stopped knockout artist Bob Satterfield in 2 rounds in Chicago to qualify for a fight against the new champion Rocky Marciano for the heavyweight title. Ezzard decided to challenge Marciano in June of 1954 in Yankee Stadium, New York. Both fighters weighed in for the fight under 190 pounds. By modern day standards, both fighters today would be fighting in the cruiserweight division and not the heavyweight division.

Ezzard came out moving well and counterpunching. Ezzard took the first 3 rounds with his accurate sharpshooting, but Marciano started going effectively to the body around the 4th round. Marciano had cuts on his face, but he kept charging forward. Ezzard fought back hard and matched Marciano punch for punch, but it was evident that Marciano was starting to wear him down by the 8th round. Marciano took the fight over in the 10th round and gave Ezzard a terrible beating to the face and body. Ezzard bravely refused to fall, and he came out in the 14th round with an all-out attack that won him the round on the scorecards. Marciano was back in control in the 15th and final round to take the unanimous decision victory. Ezzard was the only contender that would go the distance in Marciano's title fights. Ezzard received worldwide acclaim for his brave stand against Marciano and he was given a rematch in September of 1954.

Ezzard was dropped in the 2nd round of the rematch, and he was taking a beating until Marciano came out of a clinch in the 6th round with a severe cut on his nose. Ezzard went all out to try and get the fight stopped on a technical knockout and opened up another cut on Marciano in the 8th round. Marciano, realizing his title was slipping away, fought back with a fury and dropped him to the canvas twice. Ezzard could not get up before the 10 count after the last knockdown and his dreams of regaining his title were over.

Ezzard would continue fighting until 1959 losing over half of his fights and becoming merely an opponent for up-and-coming fighters. Like Joe Louis before him, financial problems plagued him, and he turned to professional wrestling to make a living after his ring career was over.

In 1968 Ezzard was diagnosed with a muscle destroying disease Amyloid Lateral Sclerosis also known as ALS or Lou Gehrig's disease. Ezzard eventually was confined to a wheelchair and passed away in 1975 at a nursing home in Chicago at the age of 53.

Today Ezzard is considered by many boxing experts to be the greatest light heavyweight fighter of all time even though he never received an opportunity to fight for the light heavyweight title.

Ezzard was a master boxer who was a quick, and powerful combination puncher. He defeated great fighters such as Joe Louis, Joe Walcott, Archie Moore, and Charley Burley. Styles make fights and 3 of his 4 fights with Walcott may have been boring from a fight fan's point of view because both fighters were basically counter punchers. Marciano called Ezzard the bravest fighter that he ever fought.

Ezzard's final ring record was 95 wins, 25 loses, and 1 draw. He won 52 fights by knockout. He was inducted into the International Boxing Hall of Fame in 1990.

Top Heavyweights of the Decade

Archie Moore
Television Boxing Guide, 1954

CHAPTER # 2   *Light Heavyweights*

ARCHIE MOORE

Born Archibald Lee Wright in 1913, according to his mother, or in 1916 according to Archie, he later took the name of an aunt and uncle named Moore from St. Louis, Missouri.

After several years in reform schools for theft, Archie joined the Civilian Conservation Core where he took up amateur boxing. Turning professional in 1935 as a middleweight at around age 20, he knocked out Piano Mover Jones in Hot Springs, Arkansas in 2 rounds.

Archie was undefeated in his first 16 fights before he lost a decision to Billy Adams in January of 1937. Archie won his next 8 fights before he lost a decision to Johnny Romero in June of 1938. Archie then proceeded to knock out Romero in a rematch in September of 1938.

Archie liked the climate in California and switched his base of operations to San Diego after his first fight with Romero. Archie returned to St. Louis in 1939 and won 8 of 11 fights but lost a 10-round decision to former middleweight champion Teddy Yarosz in April.

Archie finally cracked the top ten middleweight rankings when he traveled to Australia in 1940 and twice defeated middleweight contender Ron Richards. Archie won all 7 of his fights in Australia before returning home to the United States. Archie would claim in later years that he learned how to control his weight by a secret diet that the Aboriginals in Australia taught him.

Soon after fighting a 10-round draw with Eddie Booker in February of 1941 Archie suffered a ruptured ulcer. Archie's weight dropped to 125 pounds in the hospital and he needed abdominal surgery to save his life. At 5'11" in height Archie looked like a featherweight when he got out of the hospital.

Archie was out of the ring for almost one year before he returned in January of 1942 to knock out Bobby Britton in Phoenix, Arizona. Archie won all 7 of his fights in 1942 and won the California Middleweight title when he won a 15-round decision over Jack Chase in San Diego in May of 1943.

Archie was the number one contender for Tony Zale's world middleweight when Zale was inducted into the United States Navy during World War 2 and his title was frozen by the boxing authorities.

Archie won 8 out of 9 fights in 1944 and lost only to Hall of Fame middleweight contender Charley Burley from Pittsburgh. In 1945 Archie moved up to the light heavyweight division and defeated top contenders Nate Bolden, Lloyd Marshall, Jimmy Bivins, and Holman Williams to become the number one contender for the world light heavyweight title.

Archie lost only one of 7 fights in 1946. His lone loss was to Ezzard Charles. In his career Archie would lose all 3 of his fights against Charles. In March of 1947 Archie again defeated Jack Chase, this time for the California light heavyweight title. Archie lost another decision to Charles and then closed out the year by knocking out heavyweight contender Jimmy Bivins in 9 rounds.

The year 1948 did not start out well for Archie. Archie and Charles had to fight a 3rd time as champion Gus Lesnevich turned down offers to fight both men. Charles knocked Archie out in 8 rounds to end their 3-bout series in January in Cleveland. Archie notched 3 more wins after the Charles defeat, and he defended his California light heavyweight title against Leonard Morrow in Oakland. Morrow came out swinging in the 1st round and dropped Archie with a straight right hand. Archie went down twice more in the 1st round and the fight was over. It was the quickest defeat in Archie's career.

Archie rebounded in 1949 by stopping Bob Satterfield in 3 rounds and Jimmy Bivins in 8 rounds. Archie also won a decision over top light heavyweight contender Harold Johnson in 10 rounds. Archie closed out the year by knocking out Leonard Morrow in a rematch in December.

Ezzard Charles had moved up to the heavyweight division and won the vacant title by beating Joe Walcott in 1949. Gus Lesnevich had lost his light heavyweight title to Englishman Freddie Mills before the end of 1948. Like Lesnevich, Mills had no intentions of defending his title against Archie. Archie plodded along in 1950 with two more wins while Mills lost his light heavyweight title to light punching Joey Maxim.

In 1951 Maxim decided to challenge Charles for the heavyweight title rather than defend his title against Archie. Maxim lost a 15-round decision to Charles. Archie went to the post 18 times in 1951 winning 16 fights with one draw. Archie lost his last fight in December to Harold Johnson by decision. During the year Archie toured Argentina, Uruguay, and Panama.

In January of 1952, Archie defeated Harold Johnson in their rubber match in Toledo and won decisions over Jimmy Slade, and Clarence Henry.

Joey Maxim had lost his challenge for the heavyweight title against Ezzard Charles, and he was under tremendous pressure from the boxing authorities to defend his title against Archie.

Maxim eventually signed to defend against Archie in St. Louis in December of 1952. Archie started off fast in the fight and thoroughly out boxed and outfought Maxim to win a lopsided unanimous decision and gain the light heavyweight title in his 17th year as a professional fighter.

Archie went on an exhibition tour in the early part of 1953 before winning a 10-round decision over heavyweight contender Nino Valdes. Archie made his first title defense against Maxim in June of 1953 in Ogden, Utah.

Archie got off to a slow start and Maxim was leading on the scorecards after 10 rounds of the title fight. Archie closed strong to win the unanimous decision over Maxim to retain his title. Maxim complained about the decision and demanded a rubber match. Archie gave Maxim another rematch in January of 1954 in Miami.

Archie left no doubt as to who the better fighter was in a lopsided, but unanimous, decision victory over Maxim. This would be the last title fight for Joey Maxim in his long hall of fame career.

In August Archie gave his old nemesis Harold Johnson a shot at his light heavyweight title. Archie looked lethargic in the fight and was behind in the scoring after 13 rounds. Archie cornered Johnson in the 14th round and dropped him with a right hand. Johnson got up, but Archie swarmed all over him and saved his title with a 14th round technical knockout.

In 1955 Archie again defeated Nino Valdes in a heavyweight eliminator fight, and then stopped middleweight champion Bobo Olson in 3 rounds in New York. Archie then took his case to the press to demand a chance at Rocky Marciano's heavyweight title.

Marciano's promoters agreed to take the fight, and Rocky defended his title against Archie in September in Yankee Stadium.

In the second round of the title fight Archie dropped Marciano to the canvas with a left hook. Marciano went down to one knee and his gloves were resting on the canvas. Marciano was up at the count of 2, but referee Harry Kessler forgot that the mandatory 8 count had been waived for the fight, and he continued his count on an upright Marciano. Kessler realized his mistake at about the count of 5, and he immediately called the fighters back to the action. Moore would later claim that he lost precious seconds to attack Marciano because of Kessler's error.

Marciano started to unload his power shots on Archie and dropped him to the canvas twice in the 6th round. Moore was an excellent defensive fighter, but Rocky was still hurting him with his all-out assault in the ring. Archie was dropped again in the 8th round, and barely made it to the end of the round. After the 8th round the referee visited Archie's corner and asked him if he wished to continue to fight. Archie said that he wished to be counted out in the ring, and not quit on his stool. Archie came out fighting in the 9th round, but Marciano dropped him in a corner and Archie was too exhausted and beat to pull his tired body up before the 10 count. Archie put up a brave fight, but Rocky was just too strong for him in the ring.

Archie returned to the ring in 1956 and won 11 straight fights including a successful defense of his light heavyweight title against Yolande Pompey in England in June. Archie stopped Pompey in the 10th round to set up a fight for the vacant heavyweight title against newcomer Floyd Patterson as Marciano had vacated the heavyweight title in April of 1956. Patterson had won a title eliminator fight against Tommy "Hurricane" Jackson to qualify for the title fight. The heavyweight title fight was set for November of 1956 in Chicago. The odds on the fight were about even, but the wise guys and boxing insider's money was on Moore due to his brave stand against Marciano.

Archie fought one of the worst fights of his career. Patterson was just too fast for Archie, and he could not get out of the way of Patterson's left hook. Finally, in the 5th round, Patterson caught Archie with a perfect left hook dropping him flat on his face. Archie beat the count, but the referee stopped the fight, making Patterson, at 21 years of age, the youngest heavyweight champion in history at the time

Archie returned in 1957 and fought 6 times. In September he stopped weak-chinned contender Tony Anthony in a 7-round title defense held in Los Angeles, California.

Archie won 9 straight fights in 1958 before traveling to Montreal, Canada to defend his light heavyweight title against local contender Yvon Durelle in December. Durelle was a crude brawler as well as a local fisherman in Canada.

Archie came out for the first round of his fight with Durelle, and he was immediately floored by a huge overhand right to the head. Archie laid flat on his back and he barely got up before referee Jack Sharkey completed the 10 count. Archie went down immediately a second time from a half push and half punch. Archie arose groggy and Durelle put it to him a third time with another wild right hand. Archie, again, barely beat the count and was in bad shape when he returned to his corner.

Durelle seemed to have punched himself out in the second round and allowed Archie to survive the round. Durelle continued to rain heavy leather on Archie in the 3rd round and dropped him to the canvas like a sack of cod in the 5th round. By the 7th round Durelle was exhausted and Archie took control of the fight. Archie knocked Durelle down several times before finally flooring him in the 11th round in the Fight of The Decade. This fight may have been Archie's finest moment in the ring.

Archie gave Durelle a rematch in August of 1959 and stopped him in 3 rounds in an easy title defense. Durelle was hurt early in the fight and did not pose the same threat to Moore as he did in their first fight.

Archie won 3 of 4 fights in 1960 with his one loss coming to Italian Guilio Rinaldi in a non-title fight in Italy. Archie also took time off during the year to star in a movie filmed by Metro-Goldwyn-Mayer: *The Adventures of Huckleberry Finn*. Archie got positive reviews for his portrayal of the slave named Jim.

Archie defended his title against Rinaldi in June in New York City and won a rather easy but bloody 15-round decision over the title contender.

In 1962 Archie moved up to the heavyweight division and was stripped of his light heavyweight title by the boxing authorities for lack of making any title defenses. Archie knocked out top-ten heavyweight contender Alejandro Lavorante, but in November he was stopped in 4 rounds by the future heavyweight champion Muhammed Ali.

Archie returned to the ring for the final time in March of 1963 and knocked out wrestler Mike DiBiase in 3 rounds in Arizona. After retirement Archie, along with former featherweight champion Sandy Saddler, helped train heavyweight champion George Foreman. Archie devoted a lot of his time to helping troubled youth with his Any Boy Can program and owned a variety of businesses in his adopted hometown of San Diego, California.

Archie's final ring record was 186 wins, 23 loses, and 10 draws. He won 132 fights by knockout. He was inducted into the International Boxing Hall of Fame in 1990. He was the premier light heavyweight boxing champion of the 1950's decade. It was finally determined by checking a Missouri census that he was actually born in 1916 when he passed away at the age of 82 in 1998.

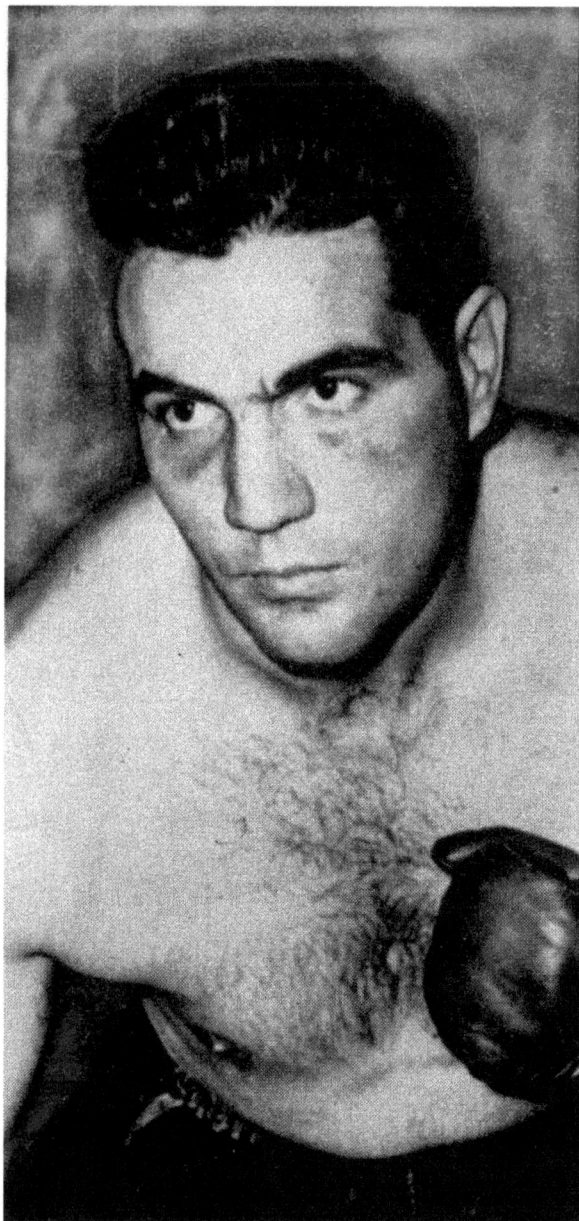

Joey Maxim
Television Boxing Guide, 1954

JOEY MAXIM

Guiseppe Antonio Berardellli was born on March 28, 1922 in Cleveland, Ohio and was later known as Joey Maxim. The ring name was based on the Maxim machine gun which was compared to his rapierlike left jab.

Joey had an outstanding amateur career which saw him win the Chicago Golden Gloves, Intercity Golden Gloves, and the National Amateur Athletic Union championship as a middleweight in 1940.

Tall for a middleweight at 6'1" in height, Joey turned professional in the light heavyweight division in 1941. Joey won 11 of his first 12 fights including a win over top heavyweight Red Burman.

In January of 1942 Joey lost a decision to ranked heavyweight Booker Beckwith in Chicago. Joey decisioned power punching Curtis (The Hatchetman) Sheppard but then lost 2 decisions to ring great Ezzard Charles at the end of the year.

Joey was stopped for the only time in his career in a rematch with Sheppard in March of 1943. Four weeks later, Joey defeated Sheppard in their rubber match in Cleveland.

During the World War 2 years, Joey was drafted into the United States Army, and he became a boxing instructor while located stateside. Some newspaper outlets reported that he was also a military policeman during the war. During the war years, Joey found time to stay active and defeated contenders Nate Bolden, and Buddy Walker.

In August of 1946 Joey scored a huge win over future heavyweight champion Jersey Joe Walcott in Walcott's hometown of Camden, New Jersey. Joey lost a couple of close decisions to Walcott in 1947, but in 1948 he beat top contenders Bob Satterfield, and Jimmy Bivins.

In February of 1949 Joey lost again to Ezzard Charles on a majority decision but returned in May to decision former light heavyweight Gus Lesnevich. In October he managed to stop heavyweight contender Joe Kahut. Joey closed out the year by winning decisions over Pat McCafferty in November, and Bill Peterson in December. Joey was named the number one light heavyweight contender to champion Freddie Mills by the various boxing magazines. Mills agreed to defend his title against Joey in London in January of 1950. The fight was held in Earl's Court.

Joey entered the ring as a huge underdog to the favored champion. Mills started off strong by going for the quick knockout, but Joey boxed beautifully and held him off with his rapier-like left jab. Mills began to wear down in the middle rounds as Joey was making the most of his punches. Joey picked up the tempo in the middle rounds, while Mills faded badly. Joey went on the attack in the 10th round and stopped Mills in order to take his light heavyweight title. It was a huge upset as Joey was not known as a knockout puncher

After several more wins in 1950 Joey challenged Ezzard Charles for his heavyweight championship in May of 1951. Joey, like Archie Moore before him, simply could not beat Ezzard Charles and he lost another decision to the formidable champion.

In August Joey defended his light heavyweight title for the first time against hard punching top contender "Irish" Bob Murphy.

Murphy came out aggressively and banged Joey all over the ring for the first 3 rounds. Joey survived the onslaught and came back strong and closed one of Murphy's eyes with his pinpoint jabs. Joey proceeded to give Murphy a painful boxing lesson and won the unanimous decision over the ex-sailor.

In June of 1952 Joey defended his light heavyweight title against Middleweight Champion Sugar Ray Robinson in Yankee Stadium, New York. New York was experiencing a record heat wave, and it was over 103 degrees when the fighters stepped into the ring to fight.

Robinson started out fast, out boxing Maxim and dancing away to avoid his counter punches. At the end of 10 rounds Robinson had a wide lead on the scorecards. Referee Ruby Goldstein succumbed to the heat and had to be replaced by another referee after the 10th round. Robinson had started to slow down by the 12th round, and by the 13th round Robinson was staggering all around the ring due to heat exhaustion. At one point Robinson missed a wild swing and fell flat on his face in the middle of the ring. Robinson wobbled back to his corner at the end of the 13th round, and he was unable to answer the bell to start the 14th round. Maxim, who was way behind on points at the time, was declared the winner by a 14th round technical knockout. Robinson retired from the ring for a period of 2 years after this defeat.

In December Joey was ordered to defend his title against top contender Archie Moore in St. Louis. Moore out boxed Joey over the 15-round distance to win a unanimous decision and take his title.

In March of 1953 Joey tuned up for a rematch with Moore by outpointing his primary contender Danny Nardico over 10 rounds. Joey challenged Moore for the title in June in Ogden, Utah.

Joey started off strong in the rematch and was ahead on the scorecards after 10 rounds. Moore had to stage a late-rounds rally to save his title with a close unanimous decision. Joey felt that he had won the rematch, and he asked Moore for another chance at the title. Moore agreed to the rubber match and it was held in Miami in January of 1954.

Moore thoroughly dominated Joey in their fight: knocking him down and winning a lopsided but unanimous decision. This would be the last time Joey would ever fight for any world title.

In June of 1954 Joey took on unbeaten future heavyweight champion Floyd Patterson in an 8-round nationally televised fight. Joey was too experienced for Floyd and handed him his first loss as a professional. In November Joey still had enough left to win a decision over ranked light heavyweight contender Paul Andrews.

Joey won only 2 of his last 9 fights, and he finally announced his retirement from the ring in 1959.

After retirement, Joey tried his hand at stand-up comedy and drove a taxi for a short period of time. Joey was also a greeter at Las Vegas casinos for a time. Joey also appeared in one nude musical, *Goldilocks and The Three Bares*, though he was not nude in the musical.

Joey was a master boxer, who had great stamina and an iron chin. He was stopped only once in a career spanning over 100 professional fights. He held victories over Jersey Joe Walcott, Floyd Patterson, Sugar Ray Robinson, Freddy Mills, and "Irish" Bob Murphy.

Joey's feats were finally recognized as he was inducted into the International Boxing Hall of fame in 1994. Joey's final ring record was 82 wins, 29 loses, and 4 draws. He won 21 fights by knockout. Some boxing sources also reported that Joey had over 200 amateur fights before he turned professional. Joey died at age 79 in 2001.

Harold Johnson
Boxing Illustrated Wrestling News, June 1964

HAROLD JOHNSON

Harold Johnson was born in Manayunk, Pennsylvania on August 9, 1928. Harold learned to box while in the United States Navy before turning professional in 1946.

Harold was undefeated in his first 24 fights, but his streak ended when he lost a 10-round decision to future light heavyweight champion Archie Moore in April of 1949 in Philadelphia. In 1950 Harold was stopped in 3 rounds by future world heavyweight champion Jersey Joe Walcott in Philadelphia. In a rare coincidence, Walcott had also stopped Harold's father Phil Johnson in 3 rounds in 1936.

Harold went on another winning streak, until he lost a decision to Archie Moore in their rematch in September of 1951. In December Harold finally defeated Moore in their rubber match again in Philadelphia.

In January of 1952 Harold lost a 10-round decision again in his fourth fight with Archie Moore. In August Harold lost a 10-round decision to Bob Satterfield, but in October he knocked Satterfield out in 2 rounds in a rematch. In November he won a 10-round decision over top heavyweight contender Nino Valdes.

Harold won all 6 of his matches in 1953. Harold defeated Jimmy Slade in January in New York, and in September he won a 10-round decision over former heavyweight champion Ezzard Charles. In November he concluded the most successful year of his career with a 10-round decision over Chubby Wright in Hershey, Pennsylvania.

45

In January of 1954 he defeated Jimmy Slade in a rematch in New York and won a 10-round decision over contender Paul Andrews in May in Chicago to set up a world title fight with light heavyweight champion Archie Moore in August in New York.

Harold fought the fight of his life and he out-boxed and out-fought Moore. Harold dropped Archie in the 10th round, to take a big lead on the scorecards going into the 14th round of their title fight. Moore knew he was behind on the scorecards and he launched a desperate attack to drive Harold into a corner. Moore dropped Harold with a right hand and swarmed all over him when he got up to take the technical knockout victory in the 14th round. Moore would never give Harold a rematch during his title reign as he apparently remembered how he almost lost his title in this 1954 fight.

Harold returned to the ring and won decisions over Julio Mederos, and Marty Marshall to close out 1954. Moore turned his attention to fighting heavyweights in 1955 and 1956 and left Harold in the light heavyweight division to fight other contenders such as Paul Andrews.

In a 1955 fight with Julio Mederos, Harold collapsed in the 2nd round to the surprise of the crowd. It was later disclosed that Harold had been drugged before the fight. Harold claimed that he had eaten a tainted orange before the fight.

Harold stayed busy in 1956 and 1957 defeating the likes of Bob Satterfield, Clarence Hinnant, and Wayne Bethea. Harold also went undefeated in 1958 and 1959 by defeating Bert Whitehurst, and Sonny Ray.

In 1960 Harold won a decision over Clarence Floyd in May. Later in the year the National Boxing Association stripped Moore of his light heavyweight title due to his lack of title defenses in the division.

In February of 1961 Harold met Jesse Bowdry for the vacant National Boxing Association light heavyweight title in Miami Beach. Harold dominated and stopped Bowdry in the 9th round to finally win the light heavyweight title after 15 frustrating years of professional fighting.

Two months later, in April, Harold defended his National Boxing Association light heavyweight crown against challenger Von Clay in front of his hometown fans in Philadelphia. Harold wasted no time in blasting Clay out in 2 quick rounds in front of his admirers.

In June of 1962 Harold gained worldwide recognition as light heavyweight champion when he traveled to Berlin, Germany to win a tough 15-round unanimous decision over veteran local challenger Gustav (Bubi) Scholz.

In June of 1963 Harold traveled to Las Vegas, Nevada to defend against veteran light heavyweight contender Willie (The Wisp) Pastrano. Pastrano was an excellent boxer, but did not have a knockout punch

Pastrano fought a very tactical fight where he would stick and move, and rarely got involved in trading blows with Harold in the ring's center. There was no doubt that Harold was the stronger puncher, but he was allowing Pastrano to steal rounds with his rapid movement and light jabs. Harold finished strongly but Pastrano was awarded the title on a close split decision. Harold hollered "robbery," but the decision stood. To make matters worse, Pastrano, like Archie Moore before him, would never give Harold a rematch for the title

Harold returned to the ring in December and won a 10-round decision over hard punching contender Henry Hank in Philadelphia. Harold had only one fight in 1964 as he knocked out Hank Casey in 8 rounds in Santa Monica, California.

Harold was inactive in 1965 but returned to the ring in January of 1966 and lost a decision to Johhny Persol. Harold defeated Pekka Kokkonen in 10 rounds in Vienna in December. In May of 1967 Harold defeated contender Herschel Jacobs and in August he traveled to New Orleans to win a 10-round decision over Eddie (Bossman) Jones.

Harold defeated contenders Lothar Stengel, and Johnny Alford in 1968, but in 1969 Harold retired from the ring because he was unable to get any title fights in the light heavyweight division. In 1971 Harold made a one fight comeback and was stopped by Herschel Jacobs in a rematch of a 1967 fight.

Harold was very bitter when he finally retired from boxing because light heavyweight champions Archie Moore in the 1950's and Willie Pastrano in the 1960's refused to give him rematches with their titles at stake. Harold was also upset that Jose Torres, and Dick Tiger also refused to risk their light heavyweight titles against him before he retired from the ring. Harold also claimed that he never received a decent payday during his entire boxing career. Some critics claimed that Harold had a boring style in the ring, and that this may have caused him to miss out on some big money fights.

Though he did not win the light heavyweight title until the 1960's Harold may well have been the best fighter in the light heavyweight division behind Archie Moore in the decade of the 1950's. His final ring record was 76 wins, 11 loses and with 32 wins coming by knockout.

Harold was inducted into the International Boxing Hall of Fame in 1993. He passed away at the age of 86 in 2015.

Sugar Ray Robinson
The Ring Magazine, June 1988

CHAPTER # 3   MIDDLEWEIGHTS

SUGAR RAY ROBINSON

Walker Smith Junior was born in Ailey, Georgia on May 3, 1921. When his parents separated he went with his mother to live in the Harlem section of New York City.

Walker dropped out of high school and took up amateur boxing in New York City. He had a friend named Ray Robinson, and he used his name to enter an amateur tournament due to age restrictions. He kept that name throughout his ring career, and the nickname Sugar was added due to his sweet style of boxing.

It had been reported that he was undefeated as an amateur, but that fact has been disputed. As Ray Robinson he was credited with 80 amateur victories with 69 knockouts to his credit. Ray won the New York and Intercity Golden Gloves titles in 1939 and 1940 in the featherweight and lightweight divisions.

Ray turned professional in 1940 by knocking out Joe Echevarria. Ray won all 5 of his fights in 1940 with 4 wins coming by knockout. In 1941 Ray moved up to the welterweight division and defeated lightweight champion Sammy Angott in an over the weight non-title match. Ray also defeated former welterweight champion Fritzie Zivic and future welterweight champion Marty Servo.

In 1942 Ray broke into the world welterweight rankings with wins over Angott, Zivic, and Servo in rematches. Ray also defeated future middleweight champion Jake LaMotta by decision.

In February of 1943 Ray suffered his first professional loss after 40 professional victories, when he was dropped and lost a unanimous decision to Lamotta in Detroit. A few weeks later Ray defeated LaMotta in their rubber match in Detroit. In August Ray closed out the year by winning a 10-round decision over former triple champion Henry Armstrong in New York City. It appeared that Ray carried Armstrong to the final bell and could have knocked him out in the late rounds if he desired.

In 1943 Ray was inducted into the United States Army and boxed a series of exhibitions with his friend, heavyweight champion Joe Louis. Due to medical issues, Ray was given an honorable discharge from the Army in June of 1944 and continued his ring career by beating Izzy Janazzo before the end of the year.

In 1945 Ray won two more fights with Jake LaMotta by decision, and also defeated top welterweight contender Tommy Bell. In 1946 he became the number one ranked welterweight contender with wins over Sammy Angott, and Izzy Janazzo in rematches. In the same year, Marty Servo had defeated Freddie (Red) Cochrane to win the welterweight title in February but injured his nose in a non-title fight with middleweight Rocky Graziano and had decided to vacate the title due to his injury. A match was made between Ray and Tommy Bell for the vacant welterweight title in December in New York City. Robinson had already defeated Bell in their first match in 1945 and he was the favorite in the title fight.

Ray got off to a slow start in the title fight, and he was dropped by Bell in the 7th round. Ray fought back and evened the fight up by dropping Bell hard to the canvas in the 11th round. Ray swept the remaining rounds to win the unanimous decision and become welterweight champion of the world.

In June of 1947 Ray defended his title by knocking out contender Jimmy Doyle in 8 rounds in Cleveland, Ohio. Doyle hit his head hard on the canvas when he was knocked down and later died from his injuries suffered in the ring. Ray contemplated retiring after the Doyle fight, but he eventually returned to the ring in December to defend his title in Detroit against Chuck Taylor.

Ray boxed carefully at the start of the contest, and then cut loose in the 6th round to knock Taylor out. Ray did not make another title defense until June of 1948 when he won a tough 15-round decision over Bernard Docusen in Chicago. In September Ray won a close 10-round decision over contender Kid Gavilan in a non-title fight.

In July of 1949 Ray gave Kid Gavilan a shot at his welterweight title in Philadelphia. The Kid came out strong and was leading the fight after 10 rounds. Ray swept the last 5 rounds to win a close but unanimous decision in a very competitive fight.

In June of 1950 Ray moved up to the middleweight division to win a 15-round decision over Robert Villemain in Philadelphia to gain recognition as middleweight champion by the state of Pennsylvania. Jake LaMotta was still widely recognized as the middleweight champion of the world since defeating Marcel Cerdan in 1949. In August Ray defended his welterweight title for the last time by winning an easy 15-round decision over perennial contender Charley Fusari. Ray made two defenses of his Pennsylvania middleweight title by knocking out Jose Basora, and Carl (Bobo) Olson to set the stage to challenge Jake LaMotta for the world middleweight title in Chicago in February of 1951 in Chicago. The fight was to be held on St. Valentine's day on February 14th.

LaMotta started the fight with an aggressive body attack, but he was tiring by the 10th round as Ray was attacking his head and body. Ray opened up with a blistering attack in the 13th round, but LaMotta refused to go down. The referee eventually came to LaMotta's rescue as he was on the ropes taking a beating without punching back. The fight was later called "The St. Valentine's day massacre" by newspapers covering the fight.

After the middleweight title victory Ray went on an exhibition tour of Europe and stopped off in England to defend his title against local middleweight contender Randy Turpin in July of 1951.

Turpin had a tough, ruffian style of boxing, and he came out aggressively at the start of the fight. Ray did not appear to be in top shape, and he could not counter Turpin's awkward style of fighting. At the end of 15 rounds Turpin was given the decision and the title by the sole arbiter. The decision appeared to be fair as Ray never threatened to take over the fight in the late rounds. This was just Ray's second loss since his career began in 1940. Ray challenged Turpin in a rematch in September in New York City.

The rematch between Ray and Turpin was close going into the 10th round and Ray had been cut in the fight. Ray came out in the 10th round looking for the knockout, and he dropped Turpin to the canvas. Turpin arose with one eye closed from the knockdown punch. Ray was known as a great finisher when he had his opponent hurt; he went after Turpin on the ropes and punched non-stop until the referee stopped the fight with Turpin in a defensive crouched position on the ropes. Sugar Ray Robinson was once again middleweight champion of the world.

In March of 1952 Ray signed to defend his title against Hawaiian challenger Carl (Bobo) Olson. Ray had knocked out Olson in 1950, but Olson had been on a winning streak and was calling for a rematch.

Olson did much better in the rematch, as the fight was actually about even after 10 rounds. Ray called on all of his experience to sweep the last few rounds and win a unanimous decision in a fiercely competitive fight.

In April of 1952 Ray defended his title against the former middleweight champion Rocky Graziano in Chicago.

Graziano came out fast and dropped Ray along the ropes with a punch to the back of his head which dazed him. Ray boxed his way out of trouble and came back to stop the ex-champion in the 3rd round with a left and right to the jaw.

Ray next set his sights on Joey Maxim's light heavyweight title. The fight for the light heavyweight title was set for June of 1952 in New York. During the week leading up to the fight, New York had been experiencing a heat wave and it was 103 degrees when the fighters entered the ring.

Ray started the fight boxing and moving, and he appeared to be too fast for Maxim as he was avoiding most of Maxim's counter punches. Ray swept the first 5 rounds, but the sweltering heat was beginning to get to him before the 10th round. The referee, Ruby Goldstein, had to be replaced by Ray Miller due to heat exhaustion at the end of the 10th round. Ray had slowed to a walk by the end of the 12th round, and in the 13th round he fell flat on his face after missing a wild punch. Ray wobbled back to his corner at the end of the 13th round, and he was unable to come out of his corner in answer to the bell for the 14th round. Ray had won at least 10 rounds on the judges' scorecards, and all he had to do to win the title was to finish the fight on his feet. Maxim who had barely won 3 rounds in the fight, was the winner by a 14th round technical knockout.

Ray was severely dehydrated in his dressing room, and he was babbling incoherently. Ray kept repeating "God willed it" and he was not supposed to win. Ray retired from boxing after this fight to go on a worldwide tour with a song and dance routine.

Ray did well for a while with his song and dance routine while he toured Europe, but due to declining audiences and his desire to return to the ring he announced his return to the ring towards the end of 1954.

In January of 1955 Ray took on veteran middleweight contender Ralph (Tiger) Jones on national television. Jones was an aggressive fighter who was the favorite of the television audience, and he had obtained a top 10 ranking in the middleweight division.

Ray had trouble solving Jones' aggressive style in the ring and he got way behind in the scoring. At the end of 10 rounds, Ray was lucky to have won about 2 of the 10 rounds and Jones walked away with an easy unanimous decision. Ray did not give up in the attempt to regain his crown, and he challenged top contender Rocky Castellani in a middleweight title eliminator fight in July of 1955.

The eliminator fight was held in San Francisco, and Castellani was made the favorite in the fight. Ray was holding his own in the fight until he was dropped hard to the canvas by Castellani with a clubbing right hand to the head. Ray beat the count, but he was hurt and used until the 7th round to clear his head. Ray staged a desperate rally in the last 3 rounds to win a split decision and challenge Carl (Bobo) Olson for the title in December.

Carl (Bobo) Olson had won the vacant middleweight title when he won a 15-round decision over Randy Turpin in October of 1953. Olson made three successful title defenses in 1954 against Kid Gavilan, Rocky Castellani, and Pierre Langlois. In June of 1955 Olson was knocked out when he attempted to take Archie Moore's light heavyweight title. Ray challenged Olson for the title in Chicago

In the second round, Ray caught Olson with an uppercut as he was coming inside and Olson dropped like he was shot and did not get up before the 10 count. Ray beat the odds and became middleweight champion for the third time. Ray gave Olson a rematch for the title in May of 1956 at Wrigley field in Los Angeles.

Ray knocked out Olson with a left hook in the 4th round to end their one-sided rivalry. Ray took the rest of the year off and made plans to defend his title against top contender Gene Fullmer in January in New York.

Fullmer bullied Ray around the ring with his awkwardly aggressive style for 15 rounds to win the title in an upset. Ray used the rematch clause in his contract to challenge Fullmer to a rematch in May in Chicago.

Ray landed would be later called the "perfect left hook" as he knocked out granite-chinned Gene Fullmer in the 5th round. This would be the 4th time that Ray had regained the middleweight championship. In September of 1957 Ray signed to defend his title against world welterweight champion Carmen Basilio in New York.

Ray was about 5 inches taller and outweighed Basilio by about 6 pounds as they entered the ring. Basilio came out of his corner aggressively firing punches to Ray's body and keeping the fight at close quarters. Ray fought back sporadically but Basilio was putting up a tough fight. Ray cut up Basilio's face, but he could not stop the welterweight champion from attacking him at close quarters. At the end of 15 rounds, Basilio was awarded a well-deserved split decision victory over Ray. Ray again used his return contract clause to challenge Basilio in March of 1958 in Chicago.

Early in the rematch, Ray cut and closed one of Basilio's eyes, but Basilio fought back hard to keep the fight close. By the end of 15 rounds Basilio's eye was a horrible and swollen mess, and Ray was awarded a split decision to become middleweight champion for the 5th and final time.

Ray and Basilio could never come to financial terms for a rubber match, and the National Boxing Association stripped Ray of his title in 1959 for failure to defend it. Ray was still recognized as the champion in Massachusetts and he defended his share of the title against local fighter Paul Pender. Pender had been a fireman at one time, and he had lost a decision to Gene Fullmer in 1955. Pender was a slick boxer, who had no real power punch.

Ray traveled to Boston in January of 1960 and lost his title on a split decision to Pender in a lackluster fight. Ray showed very few of his old skills in this fight. Ray demanded a rematch and he signed to fight Pender in June in Boston again. Ray again lost another close decision, and the magic appeared to have evaporated from his career.

The name Robinson carried a lot of box office appeal, and Ray was given another shot at his old middleweight title when he took on Gene Fullmer in December in Los Angeles, California. Fullmer had won National Boxing Association recognition as middleweight champion when he defeated Carmen Basilio in 1959.

Ray fought aggressively and flashed some of his old skills in the fight. The majority of the ringside reporters had Ray winning the fight. Unfortunately, when the scorecards were read the decision was a draw. Fullmer, as champion, kept his title with the draw decision. Due to the closeness of the decision Fullmer gave Ray a rematch for the title in March of 1961 in Las Vegas.

Ray showed none of his old skills as Fullmer bullied him around the ring to win a unanimous decision in Ray's last title fight. Fullmer won the series of their title fights with 2 wins, 1 loss, and 1 draw.

Ray, who was broke by this time, decided to keep on fighting as he knew no other line of work. He continued fighting until 1965 by beating some top contenders and losing to others. When light punching contender Joey Archer dropped him and took a unanimous decision in Pittsburgh in November of 1965, Ray finally retired.

Many boxing experts have considered Ray to be the greatest middleweight champion of all time. He was middleweight champion on and off from 1951 to 1960. He had fast hands and was a master boxer with power in both fists. His only drawback was that he tended to cut in the latter half of his career.

Ray's final ring record was 174 wins, 19 loses and 6 draws. He won 109 fights by knockout. He was a five-time middleweight champion and one-time welterweight champion. He was inducted in the International Boxing Hall of Fame in 1990. Ray passed away at the age of 67 in 1989.

Carl (Bobo) Olson
Television Boxing Guide 1954

CARL (BOBO) OLSON

Carl Elmer (Bobo) Olson was born on July 11, 1928 in Honolulu, Hawaii to Portuguese and Swedish parents. His nickname of "Bobo" came from a young family member mispronouncing the word "brother".

Carl was raised in the tough "Kalihi" section of Honolulu. He trained with older boxers stationed in the military in Honolulu, and he turned professional in 1945 by winning his first 3 contests using a fake identification card.

Carl won his first 21 professional fights before he lost a decision to George Duke in 1947. Carl reversed the loss to Duke before the year's end, and he lost another decision to Boy Brooks in Manila, in November.

In January of 1948 Carl won a 12-round decision over Brooks in a rematch, and he remained undefeated in 7 fights through the year. Carl won 7 more fights in 1949 and remained undefeated for 2 years in a row. Among his victims were Anton Raadik, and the contender Milo Savage.

Carl lost to the great Australian middleweight Dave Sands in Sydney, Australia in March and then defeated Henry Brimm in Honolulu in September. In October Carl met Ray Robinson in Philadelphia, for the middleweight title as recognized by the state of Pennsylvania. Carl was not ready to fight a boxer of Robinson's caliber and he was stopped in the 12th round. Carl would lose a total of 4 times to Robinson, with 3 losses coming by knockout.

Carl won his first 5 fights in 1951, but ended the year losing to Dave Sands again in a rematch in Chicago in October. Carl then won a couple of tune-up fights before he challenged Robinson again for the world middleweight title in San Francisco in March of 1952.

Carl did well for the first 10 rounds, before Robinson closed the show over the last 5 rounds to win a unanimous decision. This would be the only time that Carl would go the distance with Robinson in a title fight.

Carl won his last 7 fights in 1952 defeating contenders Walter Cartier, Robert Villemain, and Eugene (Silent) Hairston. As Ray Robinson had retired in 1952 and vacated the middleweight title, in June of 1953 Carl was matched with New York contender Paddy Young for the right to meet the winner of the Randy Turpin vs. Charley Humez fight in Europe for the world middleweight title.

Young was an aggressive fighter, but Carl was up to the task and he outfought Young to win a going away unanimous decision. In Europe Randy Turpin had defeated Charles Humez, setting up a fight between Carl and Turpin for the world middleweight title in New York in October of 1953.

Turpin came out fast and took the first 3 rounds, but in the 4th round Carl started to go to Turpin's body. Carl won every round from the 4th to the 12th and dropped Turpin twice during the fight. Turpin made a belated comeback and snatched the last 2 rounds, but Carl won the unanimous decision to become the middleweight world champion.

In April of 1954 Carl defended his title against welterweight champion Kid Gavilan in Chicago. Carl was too strong for the "Keed" as he won a 15-round decision. Carl smothered Gavilan's "bolo" punch by fighting in close rendering the blow ineffective.

In August of 1954 Carl defended his title against top contender Rocky Castellani in San Francisco. Carl hit the deck early in the fight, but he returned the favor in the later rounds and won a well-deserved unanimous decision from the judges.

Carl had signed to defend his title against top contender Joey Giardello, but Giardello injured his knee in a car accident and then was involved in an altercation in Philadelphia which led to a jail term. The French fighter Pierre Langlois stepped in as a replacement in the December title fight in Daly City, California.

Carl was too strong for Langlois and stopped him in the 11th round on cuts. Carl was named fighter of the year for 1954 by various boxing organizations for his 3 middleweight title defenses

In April of 1955 Carl defeated former light heavyweight world champion Joey Maxim, and then set his sights on Archie Moore's light heavyweight title. Carl even advised the press that if he beat Moore he would ask for a title fight with heavyweight champion Rocky Marciano.

It was obvious that Carl was over ambitious as Moore easily knocked him out in the 3rd round of his light heavyweight title defense in June of 1955. Carl was never in the fight and when dropped to the canvas he was unable to beat the 10 count.

In August Carl won a 10-round non-title decision over the contender Joey Giambra as a tune-up for his December title defense against former champion Sugar Ray Robinson. Carl defended his title against Robinson in Chicago.

There was not much action in the first round of the title fight, but Robinson caught Carl coming inside to him with a quick uppercut and dropped him flat on his back on the canvas. Again, Carl failed to beat the 10 count, and now he was an ex-champion.

Robinson knocked Carl out in their 4th and final meeting in Wrigley field, in Los Angeles in May of 1956 in the 4th round. This would be the last title fight of Carl's career.

Carl returned to the ring in 1957 as a light heavyweight and won another 10-round decision over ex-champion Joey Maxim. In 1958 Carl defeated Don Grant, and Paddy Young in a rematch. In 1959 Carl won two fights, including a decision over contender Rory Calhoun. In 1960 Carl entered the top ten rankings of the light heavyweight division, but he was stopped by Doug Jones in August in Chicago.

In 1961 Carl defeated contenders Rogue Maravilla, and Sixto Rodriguez. In 1962 he defeated top Swedish contender Lennart Risberg and drew with Italian contender Guilio Rinaldi. In 1963 Carl defeated contenders Jesse Bowdry, and Argentine Jose Menno.

In 1964 Carl defeated top light heavyweight contender Wayne Thornton twice to close in on a light heavyweight title shot. Just as Carl was about to sign for a title bout, he was caught cold in the 1st round, and knocked out by the Puerto Rican fighter Jose Torres in December in New York.

In 1965 Carl defeated contenders Andy Kendall, and Fred Roots. In July of 1966 he won a 10-round decision over Italian contender Piero Del Papa. In November he lost a close decision to Don Fullmer, and after a 22-year ring career he decided to finally retire from the ring.

Amazingly enough, though Ray Robinson dominated the middleweight division in the 1950's due to his popularity, it was Carl who actually had the longest title reign in the decade. Carl was middleweight champion from October of 1953 to December of 1955.

After retirement, Carl worked with disadvantaged youths and held different types of construction jobs, including elevator operator in the California Bay Area. For a short period of time, in the 1980's, Carl trained super lightweight contender Sal Lopez from Sacramento, California.

Carl's final ring record was 97 wins, 16 loses, and 2 draws. He won 46 fights by knockout. During the 1950's Carl along with middleweight contender Ralph "Tiger" Jones were two of the most visible middleweights seen by television audiences. Carl was named Ring Magazine's fighter of the year in 1953, and he was inducted into the International Boxing Hall of Fame in 2000. Carl returned to his native Hawaii in retirement and passed away at age 73 from Alzheimer's disease.

Gene Fullmer
The Ring Magazine, May 1955

GENE FULLMER

Lawrence Gene Fullmer was born on July 21, 1931 in West Jordan, Utah. Lawrence dropped his first name and turned professional under the name of Gene Fullmer and under the management of his amateur boxing coach Marv Jenson.

Under Jenson's guidance, Gene won his first 29 fights with his aggressive brawling and mauling style of boxing. Gene finally met defeat when he lost a decision to former welterweight contender Gil Turner in April of 1954 in Brooklyn, New York. Two months later, in June, Gene defeated Turner in a rematch in West Jordan, Utah.

1955 did not go well for Gene as he lost back-to-back decisions to middleweight contenders Bobby Boyd, and Eduardo Lausse. Gene rebounded in 1956 as he defeated the two contenders Rocky Castellani and Charles Humez to qualify for a shot at Ray Robinson's middleweight title. Gene took just 12½ percent of the gate just to obtain the fight with Robinson.

In January of 1957 Gene shocked the boxing establishment, by bullying Robinson around the ring as Robinson had no answer for his awkward aggressiveness. Gene went 15 rounds to win the unanimous decision and take the middleweight title. As usual Robinson had a return bout clause in the contract, and the rematch was held in May of 1957 in Chicago.

Gene was doing well in the rematch until he ran into "the perfect left hook" delivered by Robinson which stretched him out on the canvas for the 10 count in the 5th round. Gene rebounded after his title loss to beat middleweight title contenders Ralph (Tiger) Jones, Chico Vejar, and Neal Rivers.

In 1958 Gene defeated Milo Savage, Joe Miceli, and Spider Webb. In 1959 Gene defeated Milo Savage in a rematch, and Wilf Greaves to qualify for a match with former welterweight and middleweight champion Carmen Basilio for the vacant National Boxing Association middleweight title stripped from Ray Robinson for failure to defend the title. The match was set for August in San Francisco.

Both fighters fought aggressively and neither took a backward step during the whole fight. Gene was just too big for the brave little Basilio, and the referee finally stopped the slaughter in the 14th round and awarded the title to Gene. In December Gene defended his title against contender Spider Webb in a rematch in Logan, Utah. Webb made the fight competitive, but Gene bullied his way to win a unanimous decision in front of his hometown fans. At the end of the year, *The Ring* magazine voted Gene's fight with Basilio their "fight of the year".

In April of 1960, Gene defended his title against long time middleweight contender Joey Giardello. The match was set for Bozeman, Montana which was near Gene's home state of Utah.

Giardello came to fight, and in the 4th round he intentionally butted Gene in the forehead in retaliation for what he claimed was Gene's illegal use of his head in the first 3 rounds. The bout degraded into a foul filled brawl, which was very difficult to score. At the end of 15 rounds, the majority of ringside writers felt that Giardello did enough to win the verdict, but the judges ruled the fight a draw and allowed Gene to keep his title. Gene vowed to never give Giardello a rematch as long as he was champion.

In June of 1960 Gene gave Carmen Basilio a rematch, and this time stopped the shop-worn veteran in the 12th round of their rematch. In December Gene signed to defend his title against Ray Robinson in a rubber match in Los Angeles, California.

Robinson did well in the rematch as he flashed some of his old brilliance as he danced and counterpunched around the ring. Gene made the fight competitive but ringside reporters voted Robinson the winner in the fight by a 2 to 1 margin. It appeared that Robinson would be awarded the middleweight title for the 6th time until the decision was announced. For the second time, Gene held on to his title with an almost universally recognized unpopular draw decision. Due to the disputed decision a 4th fight was scheduled between the two fighters in Las Vegas, Nevada in March of 1961.

Gene was dominant in this fight and won an easy 15-round decision over the fading ex-middleweight champion. This was Robinson's last title fight before he retired in 1965 after 25 years in the ring. In August of 1961 Gene took on the hard punching Cuban middleweight contender Florentino Fernandez. The fight was held in Ogden, Utah as it appeared that Gene liked having the home court advantage in his fights.

Gene started the fight aggressively and built up a big lead until Fernandez came back strong and drove Gene all over the ring in the last 3 rounds. Fernandez could not put his opponent down and Gene hung on to win a split decision after 15 rounds of fighting.

In December Gene defended his title against welterweight champion Benny (Kid) Paret in Las Vegas. Gene was too big for Paret, as he battered the welterweight champion into a bloody 10th round technical knockout. Shortly after this fight, Paret would die from injuries he sustained while defending his title against Emile Griffith.

In October of 1962 Gene signed to defend his title for the 8th time, against the Nigerian contender Dick Tiger in San Francisco, California.

Tiger had the perfect counterpunching style against Gene's aggressive style of fighting. Tiger counter punched Gene into a one sided 15-round defeat. Tiger was awarded the unanimous decision and the middleweight title in somewhat of an upset. Gene asked for a rematch and Tiger agreed to it. The rematch was to be held in February of 1963 in Las Vegas.

Gene abandoned his aggressive style of fighting and adopted a boxing style to try and confuse Tiger in their rematch. Gene's awkward jabs took the early rounds, but Tiger finished strongly and at the end of 15 rounds the fight was close and difficult to score. The judges scored the fight a draw and Tiger held on to his middleweight title. A rubber match was quickly scheduled to be held in Nigeria in August of 1963.

Tiger totally dominated Gene in the rubber match, and for the first time in his career Gene quit on his stool after 7 rounds. Gene was a bloody mess, suffering from numerous cuts that he sustained in the fight. Wisely, Gene retired from the ring after this fight.

Gene stopped Carmen Basilio twice in his career. In four fights with Ray Robinson, he won two, lost one, and had one draw. Gene made a total of 7 successful defenses of his National Boxing Association middleweight title.

Some critics are quick to point out that Gene defended his title in the area of his hometown on several occasions and was gifted with a couple of title saving draws. This may be true, but it is impossible to objectively prove.

Gene had a hard-charging, brawling, aggressive style of fighting where he was willing to take punches to land his own solid blows. Some of his opponents, and the press at times, claimed that Gene made excessive use of his head and that he was a "dirty" fighter.

In retirement Gene raised minks in his Utah farm, and he also owned a gym and restaurant in his home state. Gene's final ring record was 55 wins, 6 loses, and 3 draws. He won 24 fights by knockout and he was inducted into the International Boxing Hall of Fame in 1991. Gene passed away in 2015 at the age of 83.

Kid Gavilan
Boxing Yearbook 1954

CHAPTER # 4   WELTERWEIGHTS

KID GAVILAN

Gerardo Gonzalez, later to be known by his ring name of Kid Gavilan, was born in Camaguey, Cuba on January 6, 1926. Gonzalez took the name Gavilan because in Spanish it means "Hawk".

Gavilan turned professional in 1943 in Havana and won his first 16 fights before losing to Carlos Malacara in September of 1945 in Mexico City. Gavilan defeated Malacara in their rematch in 10 rounds in Havana in November.

Gavilan won his next 5 fights before losing to Tony Mar in Mexico City in April of 1946. Gavilan arrived in New York in November of 1946 and won a 10-round decision over Johnny Ryan. Gavilan only lost one of 13 fights in 1947. Gavilan was kept busy as he was traveling between Havana and the United States to take fights and build his reputation.

By 1948 Gavilan was fighting the top contenders in the welterweight division. In February he lost a tough decision to former champion Ike Williams, but he returned to Philadelphia to beat top welterweight contender Tommy Bell in April.

In September of 1948 Gavilan lost a close 10-round decision to welterweight champion Sugar Ray Robinson in a non-title fight in New York City. After two wins over Ike Williams in 1949, Gavilan challenged Robinson to a welterweight title fight in Philadelphia in July of 1949.

Gavilan fought a very competitive fight and was in the lead on the scorecards after 10 rounds. Robinson, as was his custom, closed strongly in the championship rounds and won a close decision to retain his title.

In September of 1949 Gavilan moved up to the middleweight division and defeated contender Rocky Castellani. Gavilan finished out the year by defeating Beau Jack, and the Frenchman Laurent Dauthille.

In 1950 Gavilan split a pair of decisions with top welterweight contender Billy Graham and defeated contenders Joe Miceli and Paddy Young.

In February of 1951 Robinson knocked out Jake LaMotta to win the middleweight championship of the world. Robinson vacated his welterweight title, and Johnny Bratton then defeated Charley Fusari in March to win National Boxing Association recognition as welterweight champion. Later, in May of 1951, Gavilan challenged Bratton for the National Boxing Association welterweight title in New York City's Madison Square Garden. Gavilan soundly defeated Bratton over 15 rounds to win the unanimous decision and receive recognition as welterweight champion.

In August Gavilan defended his welterweight title against top contender Billy Graham. Gavilan won a controversial 15-round split decision over Graham to retain his title. Many boxing writers felt that Graham's late rally was enough to get the decision, but the judges' decision stood. Gavilan gained worldwide recognition as welterweight champion after this fight.

In November Gavilan fought to a 10-round draw with Johnny Bratton in Chicago before defending his title against contender Bobby Dykes in February of 1952 in Miami.

Gavilan dropped Dykes early in the fight, but the challenger got up to give the champion a tough fight. Gavilan received the 15-round split decision and then defended his title against the top contender Gil Turner in Philadelphia in July of 1952.

Turner started the fight aggressively coming right at the champion with little circumspection. Gavilan weathered the early onslaught and came back to stop an exhausted Turner in the 11th round of the title fight.

In October of 1952 Gavilan gave Billy Graham a rematch for his welterweight title in Havana, Cuba. Gavilan won this fight easily as Graham claimed that he injured his hand early in the fight. The 15-round decision was unanimous for Gavilan.

In February of 1953 Gavilan defended his title against television sensation Chuck Davey. Davey was an ex-collegiate boxer who was featured on television on a regular basis in the 1950's.

Gavilan took the inexperienced Davey to school as he won a lopsided fight by stopping Davey in the 10th round in front of a national television audience.

In September of 1953 Gavilan defended against the top welter-weight contender of Carmen Basilio from upstate New York. Basilio was a rugged competitor who was expected to give Gavilan a tough fight in his home territory of Syracuse.

Basilio did give Gavilan a tough fight by dropping the usually iron-chinned champion to the canvas in the 2nd round. Gavilan got up from the canvas to win the unpopular close split decision over Basilio in front of the challenger's hometown crowd. Gavilan used his famous "bolo" punch to close one of Basilio's eyes during the fight. The bolo punch was a combination uppercut/hook that the champion used in the fight. Later, Basilio claimed that it was Gavilan's thumb that closed his eye.

In November of 1953 Gavilan gave Johnny Bratton a rematch for the title in Chicago. Gavilan gave Bratton a severe beating in winning the 15-round unanimous decision. Bratton absorbed a terrible beating in the last 3 rounds of the 15-round fight and under today's standards the fight would have been stopped around the 13th round for the mismatch of skill. Bratton was never the same fighter after the beating he absorbed from Gavilan's fists.

In April of 1954 Gavilan challenged Carl (Bobo) Olson for the world middleweight title in Chicago. The odds makers gave the flashy Kid a good chance of taking the title from Olson.

Gavilan appeared lethargic in his fight against the plodding middleweight champion. Olson kept coming forward and initiating the action while Gavilan stayed on the defense fighting back with his flashy combinations in spurts. At the end of 15 rounds Olson was given the majority decision. Gavilan claimed after the fight that he had hurt a hand in training and was unable to use it during the fight.

In October of 1954 Gavilan defended his title against mob-controlled fighter Johnny Saxton from New Jersey. The fight was held in Philadelphia and Gavilan was installed as the favorite in the fight.

The fight itself was dull and boring with little action. Gavilan appeared to have done enough to win the decision, but the decision and the title went to the mob-controlled Saxton. 20 of the 22 boxing writers at ringside gave the fight to Gavilan and most observers recognized that the decision was very unjust. But nothing could be changed, and Kid Gavilan was now an ex-champion.

Robbed of his welterweight title, Gavilan moved up to the middleweight division to continue his ring career. In 1955 Gavilan beat the tough competitor of Ernie (The Rock) Durando but lost a rematch with Bobby Dykes. Gavilan then lost a decision to the hard-punching Argentine middleweight Eduardo Lausse to close out the year.

In 1956 Gavilian defeated Jimmy Beechum, but then lost decisions to Tony DeMarco, and Ramon Fuentes. In 1957 Gavilan defeated only Gasper (Indian) Ortega in his 6 fights during the year. In 1958 Gavilan split a couple of decisions with Ralph (Tiger) Jones and then retired in June after losing a decision to middleweight contender Yama Bahama.

In a career of 143 bouts, Gavilan was only dropped twice and never stopped. After his ring career was over Gavilan retired to Cuba but fled his homeland to Miami, penniless, in 1968 due to the Communist government confiscating all his property and money.

During his ring career Gavilan was named fighter of the year in 1953 by the Boxing Writers of America. Gavilan's final ring record was 108 wins, 30 loses, and 5 draws. He won 28 fights by knockout. As stated previously, he was never knocked out in his long career.

In 1990 Gavilan was inducted into the International Boxing Hall of Fame's inaugural class. Gavilan returned to Miami after fleeing Cuba and he passed away at the age of 77 in 2003.

Tony DeMarco
The Ring Magazine, June 1955

TONY DEMARCO

Leonard Liotta, known by his ring name of Tony DeMarco or the nickname Boston Bomber, was born on January 10, 1932 in Boston, Massachusetts.

Tony turned professional at the age of 16 in 1948 and won his first 7 professional fights, under the guidance of his manager Bobby Agrippino. Tony suffered his first loss to veteran fighter Jay White in October of 1949.

After losing to the unbeaten Art Suffoleta in January of 1950 in New Haven, Connecticut, Tony went on a 10-fight winning streak before he was stopped by Chick Boucher in 4 rounds on March 12, 1951, in Boston.

Tony went on another 10-fight winning streak before losing to Brian Kelly by decision on May 1, 1952. In September of 1953 Tony defeated Chick Boucher in a rematch, and then entered the top ten welterweight rankings by winning a decision over world-ranked Paddy DeMarco in October in Boston.

In 1954 Tony jumped to the top of the welterweight rankings by defeating Carlos Chavez, Johnny Cesario, and George Araujo. In February of 1955, Tony fought a 10-round non-title fight draw with lightweight champion Jimmy Carter and then challenged champion Johnny Saxton for the welterweight title in April of 1955 in Boston.

Tony came at Saxton with a two-fisted assault, landing his left hook throughout the whole fight. Tony eventually stopped Saxton in the 14th round in front of a wildly cheering hometown crowd to win the welterweight title. With Saxton's well-known mob connections, Tony had no choice but to go for the knockout and not depend on a decision victory.

Hardly recovered from the Saxton fight, Tony traveled to Syracuse, to give hometown favorite Carmen Basilio a shot at his newly won welterweight title in June of 1955. Tony was not a fighter who would dodge any number one contender and Basilio was no exception.

The fight was seen on national television, and it turned out to be a classic. Both fighters came out aggressively at each other and took turns staggering each other in just about every round of the fight. The blows that were landed by both fighters would probably have knocked out any of the other contenders. Basilio finally broke through in the 12th round to outlast Tony and stop him. After only two short months, Tony was now an ex-champion.

Tony returned to the ring in September and knocked out Chico Vejar in one round in Boston in a tune-up for his rematch with Basilio for the title in November. The rematch was to be held in Boston, and the fans expected another war.

The fans were not disappointed as the rematch did turn out to be another war and the fighters again took turns staggering each other around the ring. In the 7th round Tony hit Basilio with a perfect left hook to the jaw, and he had the champion ready to be knocked out when the bell rang and saved him. Basilio was behind in the scoring, but he came back to stop a tiring Tony, again in the 12th round. This fight was named fight of the year by all the major boxing authorities. Tony was a hard-punching tough fighter, but Basilio just turned out to be just a little bit tougher and with a little more stamina. The fight was again televised nationally and boxing fans around the United States were treated to a war between two future hall of fame fighters.

Tony returned to the ring in March of 1956 and knocked out lightweight champion Wallace (Bud) Smith in 9 rounds. Tony also defeated Arthur Persley, Vince Martinez, and Kid Gavilan to close out the year.

Tony lost a couple of decisions to Gasper (Indian) Ortega at the end of 1956 to knock him out of title contention. Tony came back to win a rubber match with Ortega in January of 1957.

Tony defeated hot contender Larry Boardman in March, but then suffered from back-to-back knockout losses to contender Virgil Akins in October of 1957, and in January of 1958 in Boston, to again get knocked out of a future welterweight title fight.

Tony took the rest of the year off and returned to the ring in March of 1959 to stop George Monroe in 8 rounds. Tony defeated Eddie Conners in April of 1959 and fought only once in 1960, losing in two rounds to young welterweight sensation Denny Moyer.

In December of 1961, Tony stopped former welterweight champion Don Jordan in 2 rounds and then defeated contender Stefan Redl in 10 rounds on February 6, 1962 in Boston. Unable to get a title fight, Tony announced his retirement in March of 1962 immediately following the Redl fight. Tony wanted to retire as a winner, and he did just that in front of his hometown crowd.

Tony's final ring record was 58 wins, 12 loses, and 1 draw. Tony managed to win 33 fights by knockout. After retirement Tony owned a bar and night club in Phoenix, Arizona before returning back to Boston. Tony was from the North end of Boston, and he was honored by a Statue at the corner of Hanover and Cross streets where he grew up.

During his career Tony defeated Paddy DeMarco, Teddy (Red Top) Davis, Chico Vejar, Don Jordan, Wallace (Bud) Smith, Johnny Saxton, and almost managed to defeat Carmen Basilio.

Tony is best remembered for his losing fights to Carmen Basilio but he beat just about every other top contender of the day. Tony described himself as a "pure slugger" in the ring, just like Carmen Basilio, and perhaps that led to some of the best welterweight boxing ever televised.

Tony received many honors after retirement, and he was much more than just a short-term welterweight champion between Kid Gavilan and Carmen Basilio. Tony's achievements were finally recognized by the International Boxing Hall of Fame when he was inducted into the organization in 2019.

Carmen Basilio
International Boxing, February 1973

CARMEN BASILIO

Carmine Basilio was born in Canastota, New York on April 2, 1927. He turned professional under the nickname Carmen Basilio in November of 1948 by defeating Jimmy Evans. Basilio was managed by Johnny DeJohn, and Joe Netro.

Carmen went undefeated in his first 10 fights before losing a 6-round decision to Connie Thies in May of 1949. In August of 1949 Carmen went on a 7-fight winning streak and defeated former lightweight champion Lew Jenkins in May of 1950 by majority decision.

Carmen won 3 of 6 fights in 1951 and then stepped up his opposition in 1952 by winning 6 fights, losing 2 fights, and with 1 draw. Carmen won his first 3 fights in 1952 and fought to a draw with Chuck Davey. Carmen lost a rematch with Davey and also lost a decision to contender Billy Graham.

In January of 1953 Carmen grabbed a decision over former champion Ike Williams, and in June he won a 12-round decision over Billy Graham in a rematch for the New York state welterweight title. In July he defended his title by fighting a 12-round draw with Graham before challenging world welterweight champion Kid Gavilan on September 18 in Syracuse.

Carmen dropped Gavilan early in the fight, but Gavilan staged a comeback and was given a 15-round disputed split decision to hold on to his title. Carmen had one eye cut and closed during the fight which he blamed on getting thumbed by his opponent. Gavilan claimed he cut Basilio by using his famous "bolo punch." Carmen's game effort made him a top contender for the welterweight title.

Carmen went undefeated in 8 fights in 1954, and defeated contenders Pierre Langlois, Al Andrews, and Italo Scortichini. In January of 1955 Carmen took a decision over Peter Mueller and then challenged world welterweight champion Tony DeMarco in Syracuse with the title at stake. DeMarco had knocked out Johnny Saxton in April of 1955 in Boston to win the title.

In a classic fight where both fighters were staggered repeatedly, Carmen finally wore DeMarco down, stopping him in the 12th round in front of his hometown fans to win the welterweight title. After winning the title, Carmen won a couple of 10-round decisions over Italo Scortichini and Gil Turner in non-title fights. Carmen then signed to defend his title against DeMarco in Boston in September of 1955.

This was another classic slugfest where both fighters were repeatedly hurt and staggered during the fight. Carmen was tagged by a perfect left hook to the head in the 7th round and was saved by the bell as he was about to hit the canvas. Carmen came back to drop a tiring DeMarco twice in the 10th round before finally stopping him again in the 12th round of the rematch.

Carmen's two wins over DeMarco were welterweight ring classics. The difference between the two fighters was Carmen's incredible stamina and iron chin. In March of 1956 Carmen defended against Johnny Saxton in Chicago. The fight was televised on national television from the Chicago Stadium.

After 15 rounds it appeared to the nation's television viewers that Carmen dominated the fight and was entitled to the decision. The judges voted in favor of Saxton, and Carmen cried robbery after the fight. Many television viewers called the television stations to complain about the decision. Due to the disputed decision, Carmen was given a rematch with Saxton for the title on September 12 in Syracuse.

Carmen decided not to let the judges render a decision in the rematch, as he totally dominated Saxton before stopping him in front of his Syracuse hometown fans in the 9th round. In February of 1957 Carmen fought a rubber match with Saxton with the title on the line in Cleveland, Ohio.

The rubber match was strictly no contest as Carmen battered Saxton into a 2nd round defeat and effectively ended his career as a title challenger. In September of 1957 Carmen challenged Sugar Ray Robinson in New York for the world middleweight title.

Carmen fought the best fight of his career as he brought the fight to Robinson and beat him to the punch repeatedly during the contest. Robinson fought back in flashy flurries, but Carmen matched him punch for punch and won the middleweight title on a split decision. Carmen vacated his welterweight title, and then gave Robinson a rematch with the middleweight title on the line in March of 1958 in Chicago.

Robinson closed one of Carmen's eyes early in the contest, and he made it a target throughout the fight. Carmen fought with just one eye open during the last half of the fight which allowed Robinson to win a split decision to regain his middleweight title.

Robinson could not come to financial terms with Basilio for a rubber match and he was stripped of his title in 1959 for failure to defend it by the National Boxing Association. In August of 1959 Basilio challenged Gene Fullmer for the vacant National Boxing Association title in San Francisco.

Carmen and Fullmer were both aggressive fighters who always came out to fight. Fullmer was just too big and strong for Carmen, and he eventually stopped him in the 14th round of a very bloody brawl. *The Ring* magazine voted this fight the fight of the year for 1959.

In June of 1960 Carmen challenged Fullmer to a rematch for the title in Salt Lake City. The rematch was a carbon copy of their first fight, except Carmen was stopped two rounds earlier in the 12th round

Carmen won a couple of tune up fights in 1961 before challenging Paul Pender in April of 1961 in Boston for the New York and Massachusetts version of the middleweight title. Carmen was at the end of his career and he simply could not catch up to Pender's jabbing and dancing that paved his way to a 15-round unanimous decision. Carmen wisely retired from the ring after this fight.

Carmen's final ring record was 56 wins, 16 loses, and 7 draws. Carmen won 27 fights by knockout. In retirement Carmen worked for a brewery company and also taught physical education classes at a local college in Syracuse. Carmen was an ex-Marine and trained his nephew, Billy Backus, who won the world welterweight title in the 1970's.

Carmen donated land in Canastota to help the International Boxing Hall of Fame break ground to open up for business in 1990. Carmen was inducted into the inaugural hall of fame class of the same year.

Carmen passed away at the age of 85 in 2012. Carmen was a two-weight division champion who was known for his tremendous courage and fighting heart in the ring.

Jimmy Carter
Television Boxing Guide 1954

CHAPTER # 5   LIGHTWEIGHTS

JIMMY CARTER

James Walter Carter was born on December 15, 1923 in Aiken South Carolina. At the age of 9 he moved with his family to the Harlem neighborhood of New York City. James learned to box at a Catholic Boy's club in New York City.

James joined the Army in 1943 and toured the world. When released from the Army at the end of the war, he turned professional under the guidance of Willie Ketchum, a well-known New York fight figure.

James turned professional as a lightweight in 1946 under the name of Jimmy Carter and won his first 10 fights before losing a 10-round decision to Johnny LaRusso in May of 1946.

Jimmy went on another 10-fight win streak before losing a 10-round decision to future lightweight champion Joe Brown in New Orleans in April of 1947. Jimmy and Joe Brown would go on to dominate the lightweight division during the whole decade of the 1950's.

In June of 1947 Jimmy held top ranked featherweight Sandy Saddler to a large draw and gained national attention. Willie Ketchum kept Jimmy busy as he had moderate success in the ring with fringe contenders until he finally broke into the rankings in 1950 with wins over amateur boxing star Wallace (Bud) Smith, and Jessie Underwood.

In 1951 Jimmy split a pair of decisions with top ranked featherweight Percy Bassett in Philadelphia, and then he got the call to challenge champion Ike Williams for his lightweight title in May of 1951 in New York City. Williams was a great favorite in the fight when considering that Jimmy had lost his previous fight to Bassett in March. Willie Ketchum had connections, but it was Jimmy and not Bassett who got the title fight. Williams was starting to go downhill, and he was looking for an easy title defense before he retired — he was in for a surprise.

Jimmy shocked everyone including Williams, and likely Ketchum also, by coming out at the first bell like a tiger and taking the fight straight to Williams. Jimmy did not let up until he knocked Williams out in the 14th round in a huge upset to take the lightweight title.

Jimmy had several non-title fights to cash in on his new celebrity and then lost a lackadaisical 10-round decision to the local Los Angeles box office attraction of Art (Golden Boy) Aragon in August of 1951.

Jimmy gave Aragon a rematch for the title in November of 1951 and belted him all over the ring for a lopsided 15-round unanimous decision. Many ring fans felt that Jimmy just held back in the non-title fight so that he could draw a bigger gate for the rematch for the title, but Jimmy never confirmed this idea.

Jimmy returned to Los Angeles in April of 1952 and defended his title against Mexico's Lauro Salas. Jimmy won a 15-round decision, but it was a competitive fight, and he offered Salas a rematch for the title in the following month in Los Angeles.

Jimmy again appeared lackadaisical in yet another fight as Salas pulled off a gigantic upset and took the lightweight title by a 15-round decision in front of his adoring Mexican fans in Los Angeles. Jimmy would later claim that Salas' cheering Mexican fans influenced the judge's decision. A rubber match was then set up in Chicago between the two fighters to be held in October.

Following his usual pattern, Jimmy fought like a tiger in the rubber match and regained his title from Salas by winning the 15-round unanimous decision. Jimmy traveled to Montreal, Canada in February of 1953 to lose a 10-round non-title decision to contender Armand Savoie. Jimmy would give Savoie an opportunity to fight for his lightweight title later in the year. Jimmy then signed to defend his title against local boy Tommy Collins in a nationally televised title fight from Boston in April of 1953.

The fight itself was terribly one sided as Jimmy knocked Collins down 7 times in the second round and closed one of his eyes. The fight should have been stopped by the 3rd round, but the referee Tommy Rawson and Collin's corner men let the slaughter continue in front of a national audience watching the fight at home.

Jimmy knocked Collins down 3 more times in the 4th round before Collin's corner men finally intervened and stopped the fight. The brutality of the fight being watched by a nation of fight fans almost killed boxing in the United States with its seemingly obvious mismatch.

Jimmy returned to the ring in June of 1953 and fought a perfect fight to stop contender George Araujo in the 13th round in New York City. Jimmy showed all of his boxing skills and power in destroying his worthy contender.

Jimmy returned to Montreal in November of 1953 and knocked out Armand Savoie in the 5th round of a one-sided rematch for the title. Jimmy looked nothing like the fighter who had lost a decision to Savoie in February.

In March of 1954 Jimmy traveled to New York City to defend his title against the Brooklyn Billy Goat Paddy DeMarco. DeMarco gained his nickname for the use of his head in the ring and he also had a flat top nose due to some of his ring wars.

DeMarco came out aggressively as was his style, and Jimmy fought a laidback counter-punching style. DeMarco would come inside and throw a combination of punches, and then back out before Jimmy could get set to throw his counter punches. At the end of 15 rounds, the judges awarded the title to the aggressive DeMarco by decision. A rematch was to be held in San Francisco in November.

DeMarco came out aggressively again, but Jimmy paced himself and fought back in flurries. Jimmy came on strong in the last few rounds of the fight and stopped DeMarco just seconds before the end of the 15th and final round of the title match. Jimmy became the first man in ring history to win the lightweight title on 3 separate occasions.

In June of 1955 Jimmy traveled to Boston to defend against the former amateur star and major lightweight contender Wallace (Bud) Smith. Jimmy had defeated Smith by decision in March of 1950 in Cincinnati, prior to holding the lightweight title.

Smith matched Jimmy punch for punch and closed strong to take the title with 15-round decision in a close and bloody battle in front of a cheering Boston fight crowd. Many boxing fans felt that Jimmy was just holding back so he could win a rubber match against Smith. The rubber match between the two fighters would be held in Smith's hometown of Cincinnati in October.

Jimmy did not fare any better in the rubber match as he was soundly beaten by Smith in front of Smith's cheering Cincinnati fight fans. This fight was a sign that Jimmy had lost a step in the ring, and this would be the last title fight of his career. In a ring oddity, Smith would never win another fight after his one and only successful title defense

In 1956 Jimmy would defeat contender Don Jordan, as well as Art Aragon and Lauro Salas in rematches. Jimmy was getting ready to challenge new lightweight champion Joe Brown when he was upset by fringe contender Larry Boardman in September.

Jimmy continued fighting with mixed success until he finally retired in 1961. Jimmy's final ring record was 85 wins, 31 loses, and 9 draws. Jimmy won 34 fights by knockout.

Jimmy's ring talents were eventually recognized when he was inducted into the International Boxing Hall of Fame in the class of 2000. Unfortunately, Jimmy did not live to see his induction as he passed away at the age of 70 in 1994.

Wallace (Bud) Smith
Heavyweightcollectibles.com

WALLACE (BUD) SMITH

The 1950's had two great lightweights who dominated the decade. The first half of the decade was dominated by 3-time world lightweight champion Jimmy Carter, and the second half of the decade was dominated by New Orleans's Joe Brown.

In between these two great lightweight champions of the decade was the hard-luck champion Wallace (Bud) Smith from Cincinnati, Ohio. Smith was born on April 22, 1924 in Cincinnati. Smith had an outstanding amateur boxing career with a record of 52 wins and a mere 4 defeats.

In 1947 Smith was the National Amateur Athletic Union lightweight boxing champion and earned a spot on the United States boxing team by upsetting the favorite: Chuck Davey from Michigan State University. Smith did not earn a medal in the Olympic Games, but he made the choice to turn professional in November of 1948 as a lightweight.

Smith knocked out Torpedo Tinsley in his debut and in his 7th professional fight he won the USA Ohio State lightweight title. Smith won his first 9 professional fights before he lost a majority decision to undefeated Paulie Brooks in October of 1949. Two months later, in December, Smith knocked out Brooks in a rematch in Cincinnati.

In March of 1950 Smith put up a good battle but lost a 10-round decision to future lightweight champion Jimmy Carter. Smith began fighting top lightweight contenders in 1951 and he drew with veteran Orlando Zulueta in July of that year. In 1952 Smith defeated

Teddy (Red Top) Davis, Miguel Mendivil, James Montgomery, and Frank Flannery. During the summer of 1952, Smith lost a couple of decisions to George Barnes in Australia.

In March of 1953, Smith came to a draw with the undefeated future welterweight champion Johnny Saxton in Miami Beach and won a couple of decisions over lightweight contender Orlando Zulueta.

After fighting a 10-round draw in January of 1955 with contender Johnny Gonsalves, Smith was offered a title match with the current lightweight champion Jimmy Carter in Boston. Carter was looking for an easy title defense and he felt that Smith fit that profile. Smith had an inconsistent in-and-out career up to this point where he could just about beat any top contender on any given night and lose to any top contender on other nights. Smith, at this point, was a model of inconsistency in the ring. Smith's two wins over Zulueta helped him to get his title shot, but he still entered the ring as a 4 to 1 underdog in the title fight.

Smith fought aggressively in the first half of the fight and had cut Carter's face up with his pinpoint punching. Carter fought back hard and also cut Smith around the eyes in the middle rounds. Smith won the last two rounds and took the title from Carter in a 15-round bloodbath. As usual, Carter had a return bout clause in his contract and the match was set for October of 1955 in Smith's hometown of Cincinnati.

Smith fought perhaps the greatest and most controlled fight of his career as he out boxed and out punched Carter to win a lopsided unanimous 15-round decision over the former title holder. This win would prove to be the last highlight of Smith's career. After two non-title fight losses, Smith put his lightweight title on the line against Joe (Old Bones) Brown in a nationally televised fight in August of 1956 in New Orleans.

Smith fought hard to defend his title and was leading on the scorecards until Brown knocked him down twice in the 14th round and closed strong to take a close decision and the lightweight title. Smith challenged Brown in February of 1957 in a return match to try and gain his old title back in Miami Beach.

Smith looked like a shell of his former self as Brown battered him into a 11th round technical knockout defeat.

Smith continued fighting through 1958 just for a paycheck and he lost his last six fights before announcing his retirement from boxing in 1959 and dropping out of the spotlight. Smith had several minor scrapes with the law, but he was generally a well-liked figure walking the streets of Cincinnati wearing his famous cowboy hat.

Smith did not make the news headlines again until 1973, when he was shot in the head and killed in the streets of Cincinnati while trying to be the peacemaker in a domestic dispute between a man and a woman.

Smith could be classified as a hard luck champion by today's boxing historians. His title reign was sandwiched in between two great lightweight champions of the decade in Jimmy Carter, and Joe Brown. Perhaps it is more generous to look at the bigger picture.

Smith's accomplishments should not be overlooked. As an amateur he was a national boxing champion and a United States Olympic games boxing representative. As a professional, he was a world lightweight boxing champion.

On a good night. Smith could beat the best boxers in his weight division. The chief problem is that he was inconsistent, and, like many fighters, he did not know when it was time to retire. His final professional ring record was 31 wins, 24 loses, with 18 knockouts to his credit.

Smith was a much better fighter then his record indicates, and he was one of the top lightweight division fighters during the first half of the 1950's decade.

Joe Brown
thefightcity.com

JOE BROWN

Joe (Old Bones) Brown was born in Baton Rouge, Louisiana on May 18, 1926. Brown turned professional on September 12, 1941 at the age of 15 by fighting to a no-decision verdict with Ringer Thompson at the Catholic High School Gym on Baton Rouge.

Actually, Brown did not win until his 4th professional fight when he defeated Kid Alphonse by knockout on July 7, 1942. Brown served in the United States Navy during the war and was the all-service lightweight champion before being honorably discharged. He cruised along after the war years learning his trade and winning most of his fights.

Brown started fighting the top lightweight contenders in 1947 and he won a 10-round decision in April over the future lightweight champion Jimmy Carter in New Orleans. In May, the future featherweight champion Sandy Saddler stopped Brown, but he rebounded and took 8 straight fights before losing to Arthur King in October in Toronto.

In 1948 Brown fought a draw with Luther Burgess and defeated Arthur Persley. In December of the year, the future welter-weight champion Johnny Bratton stopped Brown.

In March of 1949 Brown defeated top lightweight contender Luther Rawling in Chicago as part of a 13-bout winning streak. Brown won 7 of 8 fights in 1950, and finally cracked the top ten world rankings in 1951 when he won a pair of 10-round decisions over future welterweight champion Virgil Akins. Brown lost a rubber match with Akins to temporarily drop out of the world rankings.

Brown was stopped in 7 rounds by contender George Araujo in October of 1952 but rebounded by fighting a couple of draws with contenders Orlando Zulueta and Luther Rawlings in 1953.

In 1954 Brown defeated top lightweight contender Isaac Logart in March but closed out the year with a couple of loses to Carl Coates and Tony Armenteros.

In 1955 Brown knocked out Armenteros twice but then lost a decision to Arthur Persley in New Orleans. Brown made rapid strides in 1956 by knocking out Arthur Persley in a rematch in February and winning a 10-round non-title bout decision over lightweight champion Wallace (Bud) Smith in Houston in March. Brown then challenged Smith for the lightweight title in August in New Orleans.

Smith started off fast and he was ahead on all the scorecards until Brown dropped him twice in the 14th round and almost stopped him before the bell rang. Brown battered Smith all over the ring in the 15th and final round to take the title on a 15-round split decision. Smith claimed the humidity got to him and that he was the victim of a hometown decision. A rematch between the two fighters was set for Miami Beach in February of 1957.

Brown dominated the rematch and battered Smith into an 11th round technical knockout victory. Smith would never win another professional fight after the beating he took in this fight. In June of 1957 Brown defended his title for the second time against perennial contender Orlando Zulueta of Cuba. Zulueta had a reputation for cutting up opponents with his razor-sharp punches. In a vicious match, Brown finally caught up to Zulueta and stopped him in the 15th and final round of the title fight.

In August of 1957 Brown fought a draw with lightweight contender Joey Lopes in a non-title fight. Due to the closeness of the fight, Brown gave Lopes a title fight in December of 1957 in Chicago.

Brown proved to be a tougher opponent for Lopes in the rematch, and the champion stopped the California fighter in the 11th round to successfully defend his title for the 3rd time.

In May of 1958 Brown stopped the New Orleans slick boxing contender Ralph Dupas in the 8th round. Brown just proved to be too powerful for Dupas once he got up to the speed in the middle rounds of the title fight.

In July of 1958 Brown took on top contender Kenny Lane from Michigan in Houston, Texas. Brown had a hard time trying to solve Lane's southpaw style of boxing and had to close with a rush in the last two rounds to earn a close decision. Brown showed his frustration after the challenging fight by stating, on national television, "that they ought to throw all the southpaws in the river."

In November of 1958 Brown continued a pattern of losing non-title fights that had begun with his encountering Jimmy Carter earlier in the decade. Johnny Busso was the contender who won a 10-round decision over Brown in Miami Beach. Naturally Brown gave Busso a rematch for the title in Houston in February of 1959.

Brown went all out in the rematch and won an easy 15-round decision over Busso for his 6th successful title defense. In June Brown turned his attention to the balding top Italian contender Paolo Rosi. Rosi was a hard hitter, but he was known in the fight game as "a bleeder" as he had been stopped in several fights due to cuts. Brown defended his title against Rosi in Washington D.C.

Rosi came out aggressively but Brown bided his time and eventually tapped the fragile skin around Rosi's eyes to stop the Italian in the 8th round due to severe cuts on his face.

In December of 1959 Brown closed out the decade by taking on the top British contender David Charnley in Houston, Texas. Charnley was another southpaw, but Brown had gained valuable experience and training in dealing with them in the ring. Charnley did not present much of a problem as Brown stopped him in the 5th round of the title contest.

In October of 1960 Brown finally defended his title after several non-title fights earlier in the year. Brown took on contender Cisco Andrade in Los Angeles in front of the contender's hometown crowd. As he got older and to try and draw bigger gates Brown was billing himself as Joe (Old Bones) Brown. In the ring Brown, toyed with his Mexican contender and took a 15-round decision in front of the Andrade's loyal fans.

In April of 1961 Brown traveled to Earl's Court in England to give Dave Charnley a rematch for his lightweight title. Charnley did better in the rematch and went the distance with the champion. Nevertheless, he lost the decision in front of his loyal and disappointed British fans.

Brown became a traveling champion as he took his title on the road to defeat Bert Somodio in Quezon City, Philippines in October of 1961. At the end of the year *The Ring* Magazine voted to give the Brown vs. Charnley match their "fight of the year award".

In April of 1962 Brown traveled to Las Vegas, Nevada to defend his title for the 12th time against Puerto Rican top contender Carlos Ortiz. It appeared in this fight that "Old Bones" just got old overnight. Brown was a step behind Ortiz in the ring all night long. The decision was a mere formality as Brown won just about 2 or 3 of the 15 rounds. Brown was now an old ex-champion.

Brown would continue his career, but he would never fight for another title. In February of 1963 he traveled to England and was stopped in 6 rounds in a rubber match with Dave Charnley. Brown did manage to finally stop former contender Joey Lopes in their Sacramento, California rubber match in May of 1963. Brown finally retired in August of 1970 after just 1 win in his last 6 fights. There is no doubt that Brown was the dominant lightweight fighter in the latter half of the 1950's.

Brown's final ring record was 121 wins, 47 loses, and 14 draws. He won 55 fights by knockout. In retirement, Brown trained fighters in his native Louisiana. In 1996 Brown was finally inducted into the International Boxing Hall of Fame. Brown passed away in 1997 at the age of 71.

Sandy Saddler
cyberboxingzone.com

CHAPTER # 6   FEATHERWEIGHTS

SANDY SADDLER

Sandy Saddler was born on June 23, 1926 in Boston, Massachusetts. He turned professional as a bantamweight under the management of Charley Johnston and won his professional debut on March 7th, 1944 by winning an 8-round decision over Earl Roys in Hartford, Connecticut.

Sandy lost his next professional fight by knockout to Jock Leslie and then went on a 6-bout winning streak before losing to Lou Alter in June of 1944. Sandy fought a draw with Alter in a rematch, and then went on a 36-fight winning streak in July of 1944 that ended in February of 1946 when he lost a 10-round decision to contender Bobby McQuillan in Detroit. Sandy cracked the top ten rankings in the featherweight division after going on a 5-bout win streak. A 10-round decision loss to top ranked Phil Terranova in July of 1946 did nothing to hurt his standing in his division.

Sandy then went on a 15-bout winning streak that included a knockout of future lightweight champion Joe (Old Bones) Brown in May of 1947 in New Orleans. In June of 1947 Sandy fought a draw with future lightweight champion Jimmy Carter.

In October of 1947 Sandy lost a split 10-round decision to number one ranked featherweight contender Humberto Sierra in Minneapolis. Sandy then went on a 14-bout winning streak before he lost a decision to fellow featherweight contender Chico Rosa in June of 1948. After 3 straight knockout victories, featherweight champion Willie Pep agreed to defend his title against Sandy in October of 1948 at Madison Square Garden.

Sandy entered the ring as a 3 to 1 underdog since Pep had lost only once in an over 100-fight career. Sandy was the harder puncher, but it was believed by the boxing experts that Pep was just too slick for his challenger.

Sandy used his height and reach advantage to pound away at Pep, and he succeeded in dropping him to the canvas twice in the third round. Sandy then knocked Pep out with a powerful left hook in the 4th round. The boxing fraternity was shocked at the outcome, and Pep would eventually regroup and ask for a rematch.

Sandy won his next 5 non-title fights before he gave Pep a rematch for the title in February of 1949 in Madison Square Garden. Pep put on his finest fistic performance and moved in and out away from Saddler's powerful punches to take the lead in the early portion of the fight. Saddler came back to inflict some serious cuts on Pep's face, but the challenger fought through the blood and came back into the fight with his slick punching, and movement. The fighters fought on even terms to the end of the fight, and Pep was awarded a well-earned decision.

Sandy felt that he had won the fight, and he returned to the ring in March of 1949 and won all 13 of his fights. Among his victims were Harold Dade, Paddy DeMarco, and Orlando Zulueta.

Sandy won his first 10 fights in 1950 including a knockout over future lightweight champion Lauro Salas in Cleveland in April. In September Sandy faced off against Pep for the featherweight title rubber match in New York again.

In a close fight, Pep quit after the 8th round due to a shoulder separation suffered in a roughhouse clinch. Pep claimed that he was fouled, but Saddler was awarded the title on a technical knockout.

In March of 1951, Sandy and Pep me for the 4th and final time. This was probably one of the dirtiest title fights in history. The fight was so wild and unruly that the referee was thrown to the canvas in the heat of their battle. Both of the fighters were guilty of numerous boxing infractions with the fight being stopped in the 9th round as Pep was unable to continue.

Sandy went into the United States Army in 1952 and his featherweight title was frozen. Sandy returned to action in 1954 and won 8 out of 9 non-title fights while fighting his way back into shape.

Sandy finally defended his title by winning a 15-round unanimous decision over Teddy (Red Top) Davis in February of 1955. Sandy defended his title for the last time when he stopped Filipino Gabriel (Flash) Elorde in 13 rounds of another foul filled brawl in January of 1956 in San Francisco. Several local writers reported that they felt that the referee allowed Sandy to get away with hitting on the break and punching low during the bout. Some writers even went so far as to state that Sandy should have been disqualified in the fight.

After the Elorde title defense, Sandy was involved in a serious automobile accident that did permanent damage to his vision. Sandy gave up his title, and he announced his retirement from the ring in January of 1957. Sandy's final ring record was 145 wins, 16 loses, and 2 draws. He won 104 fights by knockout.

Sandy was a vicious puncher who was adept at cutting off the ring against slick boxers like Willie Pep. Sandy is considered by many boxing experts to be the hardest punching featherweight in history.

Curiously, even though he defeated Pep in 3 out of 4 contests, Pep is frequently rated above Sandy when people ponder about who was the greatest featherweight of all time. Some critics point out that Pep was past his prime when he fought Sandy, and they point out that several people in boxing circles felt he was a "dirty" fighter. Sandy felt that he never really received his just credit due to the issue of racism at the time he was fighting.

After retirement, Sandy, along with former light heavyweight champion Archie Moore and trainer Dick Sadler, helped train and guide George Foreman to the heavyweight championship in 1973.

Sandy was inducted into the International Boxing Hall of Fame in 1990. Sandy passed away in 2001 at the age of 75.

Hogan (Kid) Bassey
Boxing Yearbook 1959

HOGAN (KID) BASSEY

Okon Bassey Asuquo was born on June 3, 1932 in Cross River Creek Town of Calabar, Nigeria. He later became a naturalized British citizen and fought out of Liverpool, England.

Okon took the ring name of Hogan (Kid) Bassey when he turned professional under the management of George Biddles and Jimmy August. Bassey turned professional in November of 1947 in Lagos, by winning a 6-round decision over Jimmy Brown.

Bassey won the Nigerian Flyweight title when he defeated Dick Turpin over 12 rounds in July of 1949 in Lagos. Bassey suffered the first defeat of his career when he was disqualified in 5 rounds in a rematch with Turpin in November of 1949.

Bassey moved up to the bantamweight division and defeated Joe Bennett by a 10-round knockout to take the Nigerian bantamweight title in November of 1950. In September of 1951 Bassey won the West African bantamweight title by winning a 12-round decision over Young Spider Nequauo.

In January of 1952 Bassey took his record of 19 wins, 2 loses and 3 draws with him to the United Kingdom to pursue his ring career. Bassey went to the post a total of 19 times in 1952, winning 15 fights, losing 3 lights, and fighting to 1 draw. The majority of Bassey's fights were held in Liverpool, England, his adopted home-town.

Bassey moved up in weight and competition in 1953 and won 6 out of 10 fights. Bassey had a better year in 1954 as he won 7 of 8

115

fights, and he became ranked nationally in the featherweight division.

Bassey won 5 straight fights in 1955, and then challenged Billy Kelly for the Commonwealth Featherweight title in November of 1955 in Belfast, Northern Ireland.

Bassey had lost an 8-round decision to Kelly in December of 1953. Bassey was a much-improved fighter in 1955, and he stopped Kelly in the 8th round to win the Commonwealth Featherweight title.

Bassey found himself ranked among the top ten featherweights in the world after winning the Commonwealth title, and in April of 1957 he successfully defended his title with a decision win over Percy Lewis in Nottingham, England.

In January of 1957, featherweight champion Sandy Saddler had retired due to an injury in an auto accident that impacted his sight, and Bassey found himself paired against Miguel Berrios in a featherweight eliminator match in April of 1957 in Washington D.C. The winner of the Bassey vs. Berrios fight would then challenge Frenchman Cherif Hamia for the vacant world featherweight title.

Bassey won a decisive 12-round decision over Berrios, and he then challenged Hamia for the world featherweight title in Paris, France in June of 1957. Hamia was the number one ranked featherweight and the favorite in the fight.

Hamia started off strong and dropped Bassey for a short count in round 2. Bassey was the stronger puncher and he wore Hamia down with his relentless attack as he mixed up jabs with powerful hooks to the head. The referee had seen enough and rescued Hamia from further punishment in the 10th round after he escorted the French challenger back to his corner. Bassey became the first Nigerian fighter to ever win a world boxing title.

Bassey was treated as a hero in his homeland of Nigeria and in England as well. Bassey was successful in a couple of non-title fights before he settled down to give the Mexican knockout artist Richardo "Pajarito" Moreno a shot at his title in April of 1958 in Los Angeles, California. Moreno was a huge draw with the Mexican fans, and Bassey was guaranteed 70 thousand dollars for the title defense.

Moreno was a powerful but crude fighter in the ring. Bassey stayed away from Moreno's power in the first couple of rounds before stopping to attack him with his jabs and powerful hooks to the head and body. Moreno wilted under Bassey's consistent attack and took the full count in the 3rd round.

In September of 1958, Bassey took on former featherweight champion Willie Pep in Boston in a non-title fight. Pep outboxed Bassey during the first 6 rounds, but then the former featherweight champion ran out of gas and Bassey stopped him in the 9th round with vicious right crosses to the head and body.

In 1959 Bassey was awarded the prestigious MBE (Member of the Order of the British Empire) for his excellence in sports in the United Kingdom. Bassey received similar awards in his native Nigeria before he signed to defend his title against top contender Davey Moore. Bassey defended against Moore in March of 1959 in the Olympic Auditorium in Los Angeles, California.

Bassey started off strong and appeared to hurt Moore in the 2nd and 3rd rounds. Moore started to come on in the middle rounds and had made a bloody mess of Bassey's face by the end of the 10th round. At the end of 13 rounds, Bassey was unable to see due to nasty cuts above and below both eyes. Bassey was unable to come out for the 14th round, and Moore was declared the winner by technical knockout. Some writers questioned Bassey's heart for not coming out for the 14th round, but it appeared that the referee was also ready to stop the one-sided fight.

Moore signed to give Bassey a rematch in August of 1959. This time Moore opened up old scar tissue around Bassey's eyes, and stopped him in the 11th round, due again to facial lacerations. Bassey had had enough of fighting and he retired with a ring record of 68 wins, 13 losses, and 4 draws. He won 25 fights by knockout.

In retirement Bassey coached the Nigerian national boxing team before passing away in 1998 at the age of 65.

Davey Moore
BoxRec.com

DAVEY MOORE

Davey Moore was born in Lexington, Kentucky on November 1, 1933. He represented the United States in the bantamweight division in the 1952 Helsinki Olympics. Moore made it to the third round before he was eliminated in the competition.

Moore turned professional under the guidance of manager Willie Ketchum on May 11, 1953 by beating Willie Reece by decision in Portsmouth, Ohio. Moore took his first 6 professional fights before losing to Russell Teague by knockout in October of 1953.

Moore fought 9 times in 1953, winning 7 fights, losing 1 fight, and with 1 no-contest. Moore fought 10 times in 1954 and won the Ohio State featherweight championship, by knocking out Eddie Bergin in 9 rounds in Cincinnati, Ohio.

Moore had relocated to Springfield, Ohio and newspapers in the area started calling him "the Springfield rifle" due to his fast and powerful combination punching.

Moore won 5 out of 7 fights in 1955 as he fought in Cuba, Panama, and the United States. He won 2 of his 3 fights in 1956, and really caught fire when he decisioned top ranked featherweight Gil Cadilli in April of 1957 in Miami, Florida.

Moore went on an 18-bout winning streak which included victories over former lightweight champion Lauro Salas and a 1-round blowout of top contender Ricardo "Pajarito" Moreno in December of 1958 in Los Angeles.

In March of 1959 Moore challenged Nigerian Hogan (Kid) Bassey for the featherweight title in Los Angeles. Moore started off slow as Bassey outboxed him for the first 5 rounds. Moore started to come on strong in the middle rounds and by the end of the 13th round Bassey was unable to see due to deep cuts above and below his eyes. Bassey could not come out for the 14th round, and Moore was the new featherweight champion.

In April of 1959 Moore honored his return bout clause and gave Bassey a chance to regain his title in Los Angeles. The second fight between Moore and Bassey was a carbon copy of the first fight except Moore stopped him 2 rounds earlier for an 11th round technical knockout due again to cuts over both eyes. Bassey wisely decided to retire after this beating.

Moore won 3 non-title fights to close out 1959, but he was surprisingly stopped by Carlos Hernandez of Venezuela in March of 1960 in Caracas. In August of 1960 Moore defended his title in Tokyo and won an easy 15-round decision over Kazuo Takayama.

Moore returned to Los Angeles, California to knockout Danny Valdez in 1 round for his 3rd successful title defense in April of 1951. In November of 1961 Moore returned to Japan to give Kazuo Takayama a rematch for the title. The result was the same as before with Moore winning another easy 15-round decision over the persistent Japanese challenger.

In August of 1962 Moore returned to Helsinki, Finland where he had boxed in the Olympic Games 10 years earlier. Moore defended his title against local challenger Olli Maki. Moore made short work of Maki, knocking out the over matched challenger in the 2nd round. Moore won 2 non-title fights and then took on top Cuban contender Ultiminio (Sugar) Ramos in March of 1963 in Los Angeles as part of a boxing triple title match extravaganza.

In a brutal fight, Moore was dropped hard to the canvas in the 10th round. As he was falling, Moore hit the back of his head on the bottom ring rope. Moore arose from the canvas and was taking a beating when the round ended. Moore returned to his corner, but his manager, Willie Ketchum, stopped the fight before the next round began.

Moore spoke briefly to the press after the fight, but he collapsed after he returned to his dressing room and was rushed to the hospital. Moore died in the hospital several days later due to a bruise on the brain stem that was probably caused by his head hitting the bottom rope on his way down in the 10th round. At that point, the ring ropes contained a steel cable core.

Moore's death nearly caused boxing to be abolished in California and singer Bob Dylan even wrote a song about Moore's death. 50 years after Moore's death, an 8-foot statue of him was unveiled in his hometown of Springfield, Ohio. His opponent, Sugar Ramos, flew in from Mexico City to attend the event and speak with Moore's family.

Moore was 29 years old at the time of his ring death in 1963. His final ring record was 59 wins, 7 loses, and 1 draw. He won 30 of his fights by knockout. He was inducted into the World Boxing Hall of Fame in 1986 and the International Boxing Hall of Fame in 2021.

It should be noted as we leave the featherweight division that ring great Willie Pep was not included in this chapter as he was champion for only several months in 1950, and his true ring greatness occurred during the 1940's.

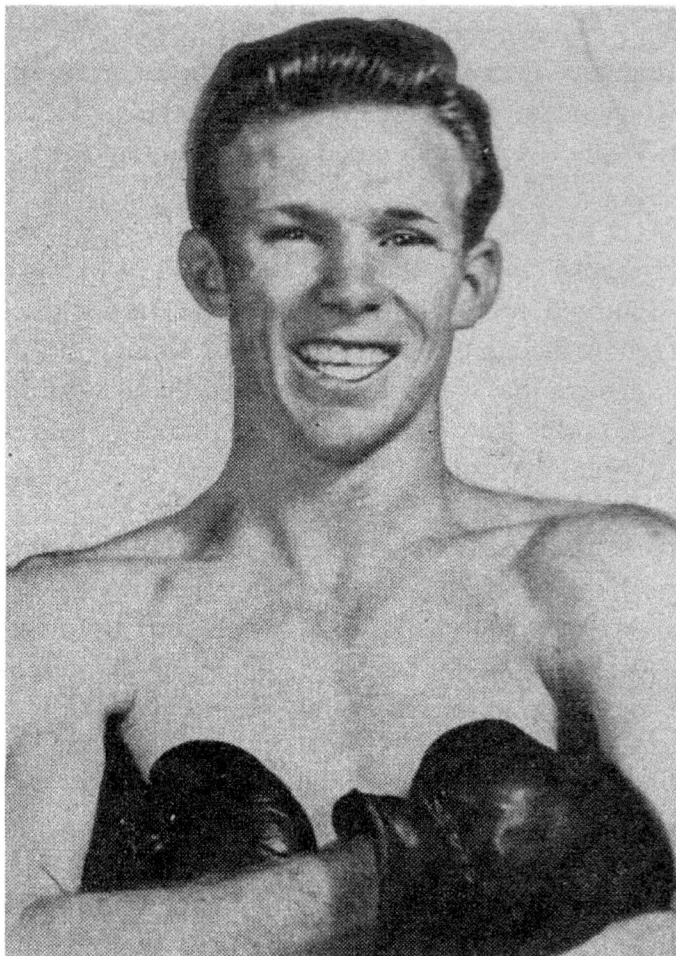

Jimmy Carruthers
The Ring Magazine, February 1952

CHAPTER # 7   BANTAMWEIGHTS

JIMMY CARRUTHERS

James William Carruthers was born on July 5, 1929 in Sydney, Australia. Boxing under the name of Jimmy Carruthers he was the Australian Amateur Bantamweight champion of 1947 and fought for the Police Boys Club. He represented Australia in the 1948 Olympic Games in London, and he won two bouts in the Olympics before retiring from competition due to sliced eyebrows.

Carruthers worked on the docks in Sydney and had a large following as he also was a product of the Police Boys Club who he fought for as an amateur. Carruthers turned professional in 1950 under the management of Dr. John McGirr and Bill McConnell, and in his professional debut he stopped Ted Fitzgerald in August by technical knockout. Carruthers stopped 38-fight veteran Ron Wilson in his second professional bout.

Carruthers won all 5 of his fights by technical knockout in 1950, and by May of 1951 he was finally fighting for the Australian Bantamweight title. Carruthers won the Australian Bantamweight title by boxing circles around the champion Elley Bennett and taking his title by decision. Carruthers received a top ten ranking in the bantamweight decision after his defeat of Bennett.

Carruthers closed out the year of 1951 by defeating 120-fight veteran Luis Castillo in Sydney in November. In May of 1952 Carruthers defeated Johnny O'Brien to become the number one contender for World Bantamweight Champion Vic Toweel's title. Carruthers challenged the undefeated Toweel for the bantamweight title in Johannesburg, South Africa in November of 1952.

Carruthers was undefeated in 14 professional fights when he challenged for the title. Carruthers, who was a tall rangy southpaw, was an underdog in his fight for the title.

At the start of the fight, Carruthers raced across the ring and hurt the slow starting Toweel with a long right to the head. Carruthers chased Toweel all over the ring and threw over 100 punches to finally stop Toweel at 2:19 seconds of the very first round to become world bantamweight champion.

Carruthers became Australia's first universally recognized world champion in his rapid rise to the top of his division. Carruthers had promised Toweel a rematch for the title in his hometown again after the first fight. The rematch took place in March of 1953 in Johannesburg.

The rematch was a competitive fight for the first 6 rounds as Toweel held his own with the champion. Beginning in round 7, Carruthers began to hurt the tiring Toweel with his left hand as he was catching him coming inside close quarters to fight. Carruthers finally dropped the badly beaten Toweel in the 10th round, and the former champion was unable to beat the 10 count. Carruthers showed the home country South African fans that his first victory over Toweel was no fluke.

Carruthers second title defense of his world title was against American challenger Henry (Pappy) Gault in Sydney in November of 1953. Gault was an alternate on the United States Olympic boxing team in 1948, and he was an accomplished veteran boxer by the time he challenged for the title.

Forty thousand fans packed the stadium in Sydney, Australia for the match which Carruthers won decisively after 15 fast paced rounds of boxing. Gault would later claim that he had fought with a broken hand suffered in training.

In March of 1954 Carruthers won a 12-round non-title fight decision over Bobby Sim in Sydney, and then defended his title for the 3rd time against contender Chamroen Songkitrat in May of 1954 in Bangkok, Thailand.

The fighters fought barefoot in a driving rainstorm that soaked the canvas. The cheering Thai crown could not help Songkitrat, as he was thoroughly outboxed over 15 rounds by Carruthers. Fighting in his challenger's hometowns never seemed to bother Carruthers performance in the ring.

Two weeks after the 3rd successful defense of his title, Carruthers shocked the boxing fraternity by announcing his retirement from the ring. At the time he was the first undefeated professional boxing champion to ever retire. Carruthers claimed that he was financially secure, and he wanted to quit on top of his game. Carruthers later bought a pub and worked in the hotel industry. Carruthers could also be seen as a referee at local boxing events. At the time of his retirement his ring record was 19 wins and no losses, with 11 wins by knockout.

After a 7-year absence from the ring, Carruthers attempted an ill-advised comeback in September of 1961. Carruthers lost a 12-round decision to Aldo Pravisani in Sydney to lose his unbeaten record. His 6-fight comeback ended in June of 1962 when he lost on a foul to Jimmy Cassidy in Sydney. Carruthers managed to win only 2 fights in his 6-fight comeback.

Carruthers passed away from cancer in 1990 at the age of 61 in his native Australia. In 1995 Carruthers was inducted into the World Boxing Hall of Fame in Los Angeles, California.

Raul (Raton) Macias
The Ring Magazine, June 1955

RAUL (RATON) MACIAS

Raul (Raton) Macias Guevara was born on July 28th, 1934 in Mexico City, Mexico. Macias began boxing as Raul (Raton) Macias at age 14 in Mexico and became a National Flyweight and Bantamweight champion. He won a bronze medal in the Pan American Games and represented Mexico in the 1952 Olympic Games in Helsinki, Finland. He lost in the second round of the bantamweight fights.

On January 1st, 1953 Macias made his professional debut by knocking out Memo Sanchez in the 1st round in Sinaloa, Mexico. About this time Macias picked up the nickname of "Raton" which means mouse in Spanish.

Macias went 10 rounds to win a decision over Chucho Tello in only his second professional fight. Macias won the Mexican Bantamweight title in his first year as a professional by winning a 12-round decision over Beto Couary in October.

In March of 1954 Macias knocked out top bantamweight contender Billy Peacock in Mexico City. In September of 1954 Macias defeated Nate Brooks by decision to become the North American Bantamweight champion. Macias became the number one contender for the World Title and demanded a title fight against champion Robert Cohen of France.

Cohen refused to defend his National Boxing Association bantamweight title against Macias and was stripped of the title, to set up a match between Macias and Thailand's Chamroen Songkitkat for the for the vacant National Boxing Association bantamweight title in San Francisco, California in March of 1955.

The title bout was Macias' first try at a world title, and the first fight outside of his native Mexico. After an uneventful 5 rounds, Macias took over the fight in the 6th round by dropping the Thai boxer to the floor on a couple of occasions. Macias dominated the fight after the 6th round, and he gave the Thai boxer a severe beating and stopped him in the 11th round with a right hand to the head. Macias became the bantamweight champion and an idol in Mexico as his fights were all televised in his homeland. Macias was a perfect blend of having solid boxing skills, to go along with his powerful punching.

In June of 1955 Macias fought a 10-round non-title rematch with contender Billy Peacock in Los Angeles. Macias had knocked out Peacock in their first fight in 1954 in Mexico City.

In the rematch, Peacock exploded two left hooks to the head in the 3rd round which broke Macias' jaw and gave him his first defeat by knockout. The Mexican boxing fans at ringside were shocked as Macias was an odds-on favorite going into the fight and he had little trouble with Peacock in their first fight.

After a short hospital stay after the fight, Macias resumed training and was back in the ring in October. Macias won his last 3 non-title fights to close out the year. Macias won a couple of non-title fights in 1956, and then he defended his bantamweight title against the Philippines' Leo Espinosa in March in Mexico City.

Macias gave Espinosa a severe body beating and finally stopped the game Filipino in the 10th round for his first successful title defense. In 1956 Macias won all 11 of his fights, with 9 wins coming by knockout. In June of 1957 Macias defended his title for the second time against another Filipino fighter, Dommy Ursua, in San Francisco.

Macias was building up a reputation as a vicious body puncher, and he systematically slowed Ursua down with body punches until the game challenger was finally stopped in the 11th round. Macias was gaining a massive number of fans not only in Mexico, but also in Los Angeles and San Francisco, California.

In November of 1957 Macias signed to fight France's Alphonse Halimi to unify the World Bantamweight championship in Los Angeles, California. In April of 1957 Halimi had defeated the deaf fighter Mario D'Agata to claim the European recognition as World Bantamweight Champion.

In the title unification bout, Macias and Halimi fought evenly for the first 10 rounds as Halimi kept pressing forward with Macias meeting him head on as the two gladiators set a torrid pace. During the last 5 rounds Halimi switched tactics and fought at long range which seemed to confuse Macias. At the end of 15 rounds Halimi was awarded a close split decision victory to become the Bantamweight unified champion. Macias seemed disappointed and surprised as his Mexican fans' cheers turned to jeers for him at the end of the fight.

Macias took a year off from the ring and returned in November of 1958 to win a decision over Kid Irapuato in Tijuana, Mexico. Macias won all 3 of his fights in 1959 but retired at the end of the year as he was unable to secure any world title bouts. In October of 1962 Macias returned for one final fight on a benefit boxing show in Guadalajara, Mexico. Macias knocked out Chocolate Zambrano in 5 rounds to retire with a final ring record of 41 wins with only 2 loses. He achieved 25 wins by knockout.

In retirement Macias acted in movies in Mexico and trained boxers in a Mexico City gym. Macias was inducted into the World Boxing Hall of Fame, but I feel that he has been an underrated champion as he suffered only 2 loses in his career. He split a couple of fights with Billy Peacock, and lost a close split decision to Halimi in a 43-fight ring career which lasted for 9 years. The charismatic Macias passed away in 2019 at the age of 74.

Alphonse Halimi
Boxing Illustrated, November 1958

ALPHONSE HALIMI

Alphonse Halimi was a French-Algerian born on February 18, 1932 in Constantine. It has been reported that he had engaged in 189 amateur fights and held the French bantamweight title from 1953 to 1955. He won the all-Mediterranean amateur championship in 1955.

Halimi, who was Jewish, always wore the Star of David on his boxing trunks. He turned professional in September of 1955 by knocking out Georges LaFage in only one round in Paris, France.

Halimi won all 8 of his fights in 1955, with 7 of his wins coming by knockout. In March of 1956 he outboxed top rated bantamweight contender Billy Peaock over 10 rounds in Paris. Halimi entered the top 10 world bantamweight rankings after his victory over Peacock.

In April of 1957, Halimi challenged World Bantamweight champion Mario D'Agata in Paris, France. Halimi entered the ring with a perfect record of 18 wins and no losses. The fight was rated as a toss-up as D'Agata was an Italian with a rugged aggressive style of fighting.

Halimi put on a magnificent display of boxing skills to take 12 of the 15 rounds and lift the World Bantamweight title off of the Italian fighter's head. Halimi did not rest long on his laurels as he suffered his first loss in a non-title fight in London in June against Jimmy Carson. Carson stopped Halimi on a 9th round technical knockout due to cuts suffered in the bout.

In November of 1957 Halimi traveled to Los Angeles, California to fight Raul (Raton) Macias in a Bantamweight title unification match. Halimi knew he was going into hostile territory as Los Angeles was full of Mexican fans who were supporting their countryman Raul Macias.

Halimi started the fight aggressively by taking the fight to Macias who fought back gamely. After 10 rounds the slugfest was close until Halimi changed his style and began boxing from long range. The switch in tactics seemed to confuse Macias enough to enable Halimi to outbox him over the last 5 rounds. Halimi was awarded a well-deserved split decision to unify the Bantamweight title.

Halimi returned to France as the undisputed Bantamweight champion of the world. In 1958 Halimi won 2 non-title fights, and in 1959 he won 3 more non-title fights before defending his Bantamweight title against the power-punching Mexican contender Jose Becerra in July of 1959 in Los Angeles, California.

Halimi made the mistake of going to war with the power punching challenger and was exchanging punch for punch until he was trapped up against the ropes in the 8th round. Becerra dropped Halimi twice and the French champion was counted out. In February of 1960 Halimi returned to Los Angeles to try and regain is title against Becerra in a rematch.

Becerra overpowered Halimi again, this time stopping him in the 9th round. Halimi just seemed to not have enough firepower to hold Becerra off in the ring. Halimi returned to Paris, and in April he won a 10-round decision over Louis Poncy. In September Halimi fought a rematch with Jimmy Carson in Algiers. This time around, Halimi gained revenge by stopping Carson in the 9th round.

In October of 1960 Halimi took on Freddie Gilroy in London for the European version of the World Bantamweight title. Halimi showed flashes of his old boxing skills by winning a convincing 15-

round decision over Gilroy to become a 2-time recognized World Bantamweight champion.

In May of 1961 Halimi lost his version of the bantamweight title when he lost a 15-round decision to Irishman Johnny Caldwell in London, England. In October Halimi challenged Caldwell to a rematch for the bantamweight title in London. Caldwell again defeated Halimi by a 15-round decision to keep his title.

In June of 1962 Halimi, traveled to Tel-Aviv, Israel to challenge Piero Rollo for the European version of the bantamweight title. Halimi walked away with a 15-round decision over the Italian to become a 3-time recognized world bantamweight title holder.

In October Halimi traveled to Italy to challenge Rollo for the title in a rematch. Rollo was given the 15 round decision and the title. This would be the last title fight in Halimi's career.

In 1963 Halimi fought twice. He won one fight and fought one draw. Halimi retired in 1964 after suffering two consecutive decision loses. His final ring record was 42 wins, 8 loses, and 1 draw. He won half of his 42 fights by achieving 21 knockouts.

In the 1960s Halimi was a cafe owner in Vincennes, France as well as a trainer for the French National Sports Institute. In 1989 Halimi was inducted into the International Jewish Sports Hall of Fame.

Halimi suffered from Alzheimers disease towards the end of his life, and he passed away in 2006 from pneumonia in France. He was 74 years old at the time of his death.

In 2009 Halimi was inducted into the World Boxing Hall of Fame. He will be remembered as a well-schooled international amateur boxing champion, as well as a 3-time world professional bantamweight boxing champion.

Pascual Perez
The Ring Magazine, November 1978

CHAPTER # 8   FLYWEIGHTS

PASCUAL PEREZ

Pascual Perez was born on May 4, 1926 in Mendoza, Argentina. Perez, who was only 4'11" in height, was short even for a flyweight. In the ring he was a terror, and he won the Olympic Gold medal in the flyweight division in the 1948 Olympic Games held in London, England.

When Perez failed to make the Argentine Olympic boxing team in 1952, he turned professional by knocking out Jose Ciorino in 5 rounds in Gerli, Argentina. Perez defeated challenger Jorge Flores in December with a knockout in 3 rounds.

Perez won all 8 of his fights in 1953, including a win over Marcello Quiroga in November for the Argentine Flyweight title. In January of 1954 Perez successfully defended his flyweight title against Nestor Rojas by a 2-round knockout.

In July of 1954 Perez took an unbeaten record of 23 wins and no defeats into the ring with him to fight World Champion Yoshio Shirai in a non-title fight in Buenos Aires, Argentina. Perez did well in the non-title fight and held the champion to a draw. After the fight, Shirai agreed to defend his world title against Perez in November in Tokyo, Japan.

In the title fight Perez knocked the champion down in the 2nd, and 12th rounds. Shirai was all but out on his feet at the end of 15 rounds. Perez was awarded the unanimous decision and the world flyweight title. Perez became Argentina's first world boxing champion and the smallest flyweight to ever hold the crown.

In May of 1955, Perez returned to Tokyo to give Shirai a rematch for the title. Perez proved his superiority over Shirai by knocking him out in the 5th round of their third and final fight.

In January of 1956 Perez won a unanimous decision over Leo Espinosa in Buenos Aires for his second successful title defense. In June of 1956 Perez traveled to Montevideo, Uruguay to knock out contender Oscar Suarez in 11 one-sided rounds.

In August of 1956 Perez was scheduled to fight Ricardo Valdez in Tandil, Argentina in a non-title fight. Since both fighters came under the flyweight limit of 112 pounds, the fight automatically became a title fight. Valdez brought a record of 0 wins and 2 loses into the title fight. Perez toyed with Valdez for 4 rounds to give the fans a show before knocking him out in the 5th round. Valdez retired with a ring record of 3 wins, and 19 loses.

It was difficult for Perez to find opponents in Argentina who weighed under 112 pounds, and he fought many non-title fights. When Perez was finally able to find an opponent who could make 112 pounds, it became a title fight.

In March of 1957 Perez returned to Buenos Aires to knock out contender Dai Dower in one quick round. It seemed that none of the flyweights could stand up to Perez's power.

In December of 1957 Perez returned to the ring to knock out the Spanish top contender Young Martin in 3 rounds. Martin was the European flyweight champion, but he proved to be no competition for the powerful champion.

In April of 1958 Perez traveled to Caracas, Venezuela to take on Venezuelan flyweight champion Ramon Arias. In a surprise Perez had to fight hard to win a unanimous decision against the game Venezuelan who was fighting in front of a hometown crowd.

In December Perez had to go the 15-round distance for the second time in a row when he took a decision over local contender Dommy Ursua in Manila in another successful title defense.

It was becoming increasingly difficult for Perez to find quality opponents and he had to go on the road to defend his title. Perez was also not drawing huge crowds in Buenos Aires for his title defenses.

In January of 1959 Perez lost his first fight of his career when he lost a non-title 10-round decision to Japanese fighter Sadao Yaoita in Tokyo. In February Perez won a 10-round non-title decision over Kenji Yonekura in Tokyo. In August Perez defended his title against Yonekura and won an easy 15-round decision in the rematch. In November of 1959 Perez traveled to Osaka, Japan to give contender Sadao Yaoita a rematch for the title.

Perez avenged his earlier defeat by knocking Yaoita out in the 13th round of their hard-fought title fight. In April of 1960 Perez traveled to Thailand to defend his title against top contender Pone Kingpetch. Kingpetch won in an upset 15-round decision to take the flyweight title from Perez.

Kingpetch gave Perez a rematch for the title in Los Angeles, California in 1960. Kingpetch overpowered Perez and won the rematch by an 8-round technical knockout. This would be the last time Perez was involved in a title fight.

Perez returned to Argentina and remained active in 1961 and 1962 by winning over 20 straight fights, but he was unable to get a title fight with any champions. After suffering two consecutive loses, Perez retired from the ring in April of 1964 with a final ring record of 84 wins, 7 loses, and 1 draw. He won 57 fights by knockout. Perez passed away in 1977 at the age of 50.

There is no doubt that Perez was the dominant international flyweight champion during the 1950's decade. Perez, along with Carlos Monzon, are considered by many writers to be the best boxers to ever come out of Argentina. Perez was inducted into the International Boxing Hall of Fame in 1995.

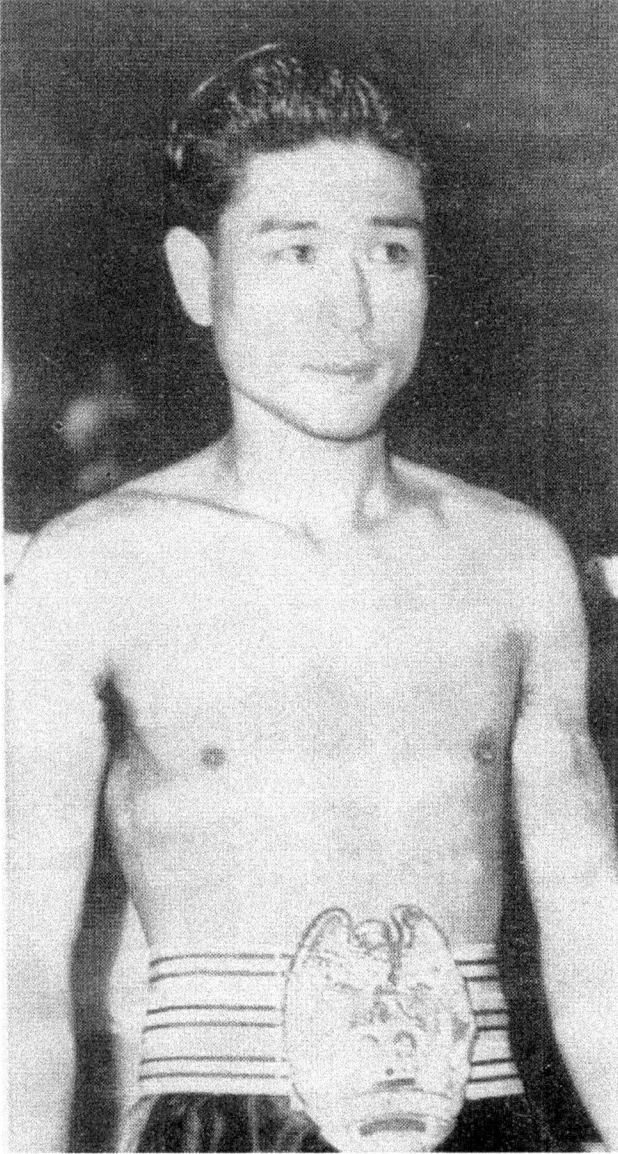

Yoshiro Shirai
Television Boxing Guide, 1954

YOSHIRO SHIRAI

Yoshio Shirai was born on November 25, 1923 in Tokyo, Japan. Standing 5'6" in height Shirai was tall for a flyweight. Shirai turned professional in 1943 and won 8 matches before he was drafted into the Japanese Imperial Army during World War 2.

Shirai resumed his boxing career in 1946 after the end of the World War. Shirai was having mixed success in the ring until he met Professor Alvin R. Cahn who was working with the American occupation forces in 1948.

Cahn had no previous experience training boxers, but he changed Shirai's aggressive style of fighting to a more cerebral slick boxing style which included counter punching.

By 1948 Shirai had recovered from his war wounds and sciatica, and under Cahn's guidance he went undefeated in 1948 with 5 wins and 1 draw. By 1949 Shirai was fighting 10-round main events in Japan and he won the Japanese Flyweight title in January by knocking out Yochiro Hanada in 5 rounds in Tokyo.

Shirai defended his flyweight title in June by winning a 10-round decision over Noboru Kushida in Tokyo. In December Shirai defended his Japanese title for the second time against challenger Hiroshi Horiguchi. Shirai easily retained his title by winning an easy 10-round decision over his challenger.

1950 was another undefeated boxing year for Shirai, as he retained his bantamweight title in May with a 10-round decision over

Yochiro Hanada, and in June with another 10-round decision over Hideo Kajima.

In October of 1950 Shirai defended his Japanese Bantamweight title against Takashi Seno in another 10-round decision. By the end of the year, Shirai went undefeated in 10 contests and had 3 successful title defenses.

Shirai stepped up to world class competition in 1951. He lost his Japanese Bantamweight title on a dubious 8-round disqualification in March against Hidemasa Nagashima in Tokyo. Shirai obtained a rematch with Nagashima in September and regained the title with a one-sided 10-round decision.

In October Shirai flashed his power and successfully defended his title by a 6-round knockout over Takahisa Horiguchi. In December Shirai became the top contender for the world flyweight title when he knocked out world champion Dado Marino in 7 rounds of a non-title fight in Honolulu Hawaii.

In May of 1952 Shirai challenged Marino for the world title in a rematch held in Tokyo. Shirai totally outclassed Marino in front of a packed house to win the unanimous decision and become world champion. Shirai became the Japanese's first world champion, and he gave his followers a much needed something to cheer about since the end of the second world war in 1945.

In November Shirai gave Marino a chance to regain his title in Tokyo. The outcome of the match was the same as their second encounter as Shirai out-boxed and out-punched the former world champion for the full 15 rounds.

In May of 1954 Shirai defended against Filipino Leo Espinosa in Tokyo. Espinosa was a legitimate top ten contender for the title in the mid 1950's and he made Shirai work hard to gain the 15-round unanimous decision.

In July of 1954 Shirai traveled to Buenos Aires, Argentina and fought a 10-round non-title fight to draw with top contender Pascual Perez. Some ring observers felt that Shirai eased up in the fight to build up the gate for a title defense against Perez in Tokyo.

In November of 1954 Perez challenged Shirai for the world flyweight title in Tokyo. Perez proved the ring experts wrong by taking Shirai's title by 15-round decision. In May of 1955 Perez returned to Tokyo to give Shirai a rematch for the title.

Perez completely dominated Shirai and knocked him out in the 5th round of a one-sided fight. Shirai immediately retired from boxing after this fight. Shirai retired with a final ring record of 46 wins, 8 loses, and 4 draws. He won 18 fights by knockout.

After boxing, Shirai became a popular sports commentator in his native Japan and owned several businesses that included a gym. In 1977 Shirai was inducted into Ring Magazine's Hall of Fame. Shirai passed away in 2003 at the age of 80 in Japan.

Dado Marino
The Ring Magazine, August 1950

DADO MARINO

Salvador (Dado) Marino was born In Hawaii on October 15, 1915 in the then Territory of Hawaii to Filipino parents. Marino turned professional in June in 1941 with the famous "Sad" Sam Ichinose as his manager and promoter.

Marino won his professional debut when he knocked out Paul Francis in Honolulu. Marino won all of his first eleven fights, with 8 wins coming by knockout. All of Marino's fights were promoted by Ichinose in Honolulu.

Marino did not fight again until January of 1942 after the bombing of Pearl Harbor. In January of 1942 Marino won a decision over Charley Higa. Marino won all 4 of his fights in 1942, including 2 wins by knockout.

Marino had an up and down year in 1943, winning only 3 of 6 fights and getting stopped by David Kong Young in 8 rounds in May. Marino turned his career around in 1944, winning all 7 of his fights, including 3 by knockout.

In April, Marino won a 12-round decision over Alfred Chavez to annex the Hawaii Flyweight title. This win made Marino one of the top main event fighters in Hawaii. In 1945 Marino, under the direction of Ichinose, continued to climb up the fistic ladder as he won 3 of 5 fights with 1 loss and 1 draw. His lone loss was to his old nemesis David Kong Young by decision in February.

Marino won 6 of his 7 fights in 1946 as he graduated into the 10-round main event status on the boxing cards. He reversed his only loss when he won a decision over Alfred Chavez in Honolulu.

Marino entered the top 10 rankings in the flyweight division as he traveled outside of Hawaii for the first time to take on Irishman Rinty Monaghan in Glasgow, Scotland. In the fight between two top contenders in July of 1947, Marino won a disqualification in the 9th round when Monaghan appeared ready to lose the fight. Marino then challenged Monaghan for a world flyweight title fight in London, England in October of 1947. Marino put up a good fight in his first title fight, but Monaghan was given the 15-round decision and the title.

Marino returned to the ring in April of 1948 and won a 10-round decision over Mike Bernal, to keep his top ten flyweight ranking. Marino won 8 out of 9 fights in 1948 losing only to the fringe contender Cecil Schoonmaker in May in San Francisco, California.

In March of 1949 Marino moved up in weight and Ichinose was able to get him a bantamweight title fight with champion Manuel Ortiz in Honolulu. Marino made a game effort, but Ortiz was too big and strong for him and took the 15-round decision.

Marino returned to the ring in July and won his next four fights before traveling to Manila and to take on Tirso Del Rosario in September. Del Rosario stopped Marino in 5 rounds. Marino asked for a rematch and then lost a 10-round decision to Del Rosario in December to close out a disastrous year in the ring.

Rinty Monaghan retired as champion after fighting a draw with Terry Allen in September of 1949. Allen then defeated Honore Pratesi in April of 1950 for the vacant flyweight title in London.

Coming off a loss to Ortiz and two losses to Del Rosario, Marino was all but unranked and a decided underdog when he challenged Terry Allen for the world flyweight title in August of 1950 in Honolulu.

Marino finally reached his potential as he shockingly won the 15-round unanimous decision over Allen to become the world flyweight champion. Ichinose's faith in Marino was finally justified as Marino became the first world champion to come from the then territory of Hawaii. Marino won 3 non-title fights in 1950 to close out his best year in professional boxing.

In November of 1951 Terry Allen arrived in Honolulu to claim his promised rematch for the title. Allen tried hard but Marino was up to the task as he again won a unanimous 15-round decision to keep his title in front of a capacity house full of loyal fans in Honolulu.

In December of 1951 Japan's top contender Yoshio Shirai came to Honolulu and dropped Marino 6 times to stop him in the 7th round of their non-title match. Marino then traveled to Japan in May of 1952 to defend his title against Shirai.

Marino lasted the 15-round distance, but he lost his title on a unanimous decision to Shirai in front of a packed Tokyo audience. Shirai in turn, gave Marino a rematch for the title in Tokyo in November. Marino lost another unanimous decision to Shirai and immediately announced his retirement from the ring.

Marino's final ring record was 57 wins, 14 loses, and 3 draws, He won 21 fights by knockout. After retirement, Marino was inducted into the Hawaii Sports Hall of Fame. Marino passed away at the age of 74 in Gardena, California in 1989.

Marciano drives Moore in the ropes in the September 1955
title fight
The Ring Magazine, November 1955

CHAPTER # 9   FIGHTER OF THE DECADE

ROCKY MARCIANO

In the 1950's the Heavyweight boxing champion was considered the best and most important fighter in the world. Rocky Marciano fit that profile to a tee. It was the age of tranquility and Rocky was the well-respected clean-living champion that the public demanded of their heavyweight boxing champions.

Joe Louis was looked upon as the best fighter in boxing through the 1930's and into the late 1940's. Jersey Joe Walcott and Ezzard Charles simply did not capture the public's profile of what a great champion should be.

The public never really attached themselves to Walcott and Charles "safety first" counter-punching style of boxing. Though Walcott and Charles were great boxers, who could punch when necessary, the public did not swarm to the fights until Marciano came along.

Marciano won the title in dramatic fashion with a come-from-behind knockout of Walcott in September of 1952 in Philadelphia. The fight had all the elements of a made for television spectacle of excitement. The old champion started off fast knocking the young challenger down in the early rounds. The old champion was ahead on points and fighting the best fight of his life until the powerful challenger, behind on points, uncorked a straight right hand in the

13th round that caused the old champion to crumble to the ground in sections to take the 10 count on the canvas without stirring a muscle.

Marciano made quick work of Walcott in a rematch in February of 1953 in Chicago. Marciano hit Walcott with an inside uppercut that most fans and the press did not have a chance to see. Walcott went down flat on his back with his feet flying up in the air. Walcott appeared disoriented and missed getting up before the 10 count. He retired immediately after this fight. After that victory, Marciano still had unfinished business with heavyweight contender Roland LaStarza. Marciano and LaStarza fought in 1950 and Marciano was lucky to eke out a razor-thin split decision victory. The 1950 fight with LaStarza was the closest Marciano came to ever losing a fight. Marciano had stated that he would never feel like a true champion until he erased the public's opinion as to who really won their first fight.

The rematch for the title took place at the Polo Grounds in New York in September of 1953. LaStarza had won 15 of 17 fights after his loss to Marciano in 1950, and he had reversed both of his defeats. LaStarza had won a 10-round decision title eliminator over Rex Layne in February of 1953 to secure his title shot.

Marciano came out slow in this fight and, as in their previous encounter, he was behind on points after 6 rounds. In the 7th round Marciano woke up to hammer LaStarza all over the ring: breaking blood vessels in his arms and putting welts all over his body. Marciano finally dropped LaStarza in the 11th round, and the referee rescued him from further punishment shortly after that. LaStarza stated after the fight that Marciano was five thousand times better than he was in their first fight. LaStarza was never the same after the beating he took from Marciano.

In June of 1954 Marciano won a bruising 15-round unanimous decision over former champion Ezzard Charles. Charles came to fight and was probably ahead in the scoring after 10 rounds.

Marciano got into high gear and swept the 11th, 12th, and 13th rounds with a non-stop punching attack. Somehow Charles came back to take the 14th round, and then he somehow survived a brutal assault from Marciano in the 15th round to finish the fight on his feet.

In September of 1954 Marciano gave Charles a rematch. Marciano dropped Charles in the 2nd round but suffered a severely sliced nostril coming out of a clinch in the 6th round. Marciano dropped and stopped Charles in the 8th round, just moments before the fight was going to be stopped due to Marciano's nose injury.

In May of 1955 Marciano took on blown-up light heavyweight contender Don Cockell from England. Cockell was pudgy and did not have a lot of power, but he was resilient and had defeated some top contenders, including Roland LaStarza. The fight was held in San Francisco to attract Marciano's Italian fans.

Marciano eventually stopped Cockell in the 9th round of a sloppy fight. Marciano hit low and even hit Cockell once when his knees had already touched the canvas. Cockell could take a lot of punishment, but the referee had seen enough and stopped the one-sided slaughter to save him from further punishment. Marciano then took on the challenge of light heavyweight champion Archie Moore in September in New York. Moore drummed up a lot of publicity in building up the fight, and both fighters would reap the financial rewards of Moore ballyhooing the fight.

Like Walcott, Moore dropped Marciano early in the fight only to have the champion wear him down and stop him in the 9th round. Moore put up a game fight, but Marciano was just too strong and had too much stamina for the old "Mongoose".

After 6 successful title defenses, Marciano retired as the undefeated heavyweight champion of the world in a press conference in May of 1956. Marciano's final ring record was a perfect 49 wins with 0 loses. He obtained 43 won fights by knockout. During his career Marciano never ducked any of his challengers to the throne. Some writers would later claim "who did Marciano ever beat?" The answer would be that he beat everybody put in front of him during his ring career. Famous fight trainer and boxing personality Angelo Dundee once said of Marciano, that he "simply was the best of his era."

After retirement Marciano met several times with President Dwight D. Eisenhower during the decade and was a regular on such television shows as What's My Line, and the Ed Sullivan show. Behind the scenes Marciano was finding it tougher to fight with recurring back problems and his financial disputes with manager Al Weill.

Other serious contenders for the Fighter of the Decade honors included Light Heavyweight champion Archie Moore, and Middleweight champion Sugar Ray Robinson. Moore was Light Heavyweight champion from 1952 to 1960, however he lost two heavyweight title fights during the decade, one to Rocky Marciano in 1955, and then Floyd Patterson in 1956. Similarly, Sugar Ray Robinson was the middleweight champion of the world on and off from 1951 to 1959. While Robinson was a five-time middleweight champion he also lost his middleweight title four times. Robinson first lost his title to Randy Turpin in 1951, and next to Gene Fullmer, and then to Carmen Basilio in 1957. Robinson lost his title for the final time to Paul Pender in 1960. In the final analysis, Rocky's undefeated record as Heavyweight champion of the world made him a clear choice for the Fighter of the Decade.

With the advent of television, and many people being able to afford them in their household, boxing was seen at least 3 times during the week. Many residents would sit by their black and white Motorola television sets and watch the Monday, Wednesday, and Friday night fights on television. As stated previously, the popularity of the heavyweight champion of the world was only rivaled by the President of the United States. In that sense, Rocky Marciano and

Dwight D. Eisenhower were the two most known icons of the decade.

WORLD'S
LIGHT HEAVYWEIGHT
CHAMPIONSHIP

MONTREAL, CANADA
DECEMBER 10, 1958

ARCHIE
MOORE
VS.
YVON
DURELLE

Archie Moore flat on his back in the first round
Great Moments in Boxing Winter 1970

CHAPTER # 10   FIGHT OF THE DECADE

ARCHIE MOORE VS. YVON DURELLE

In my recent book, *Boxing's Super 70's*, I listed the Muhammed Ali v. Joe Frazier 1 fight in 1971 as the fight of the decade. Not only was the fight for the heavyweight championship but it culminated in Ali's return to the ring to attempt to regain the Heavyweight Championship that was stripped from him in 1967 by various boxing bodies.

The most exciting fight of the decade was, by far, the George Foreman vs. Ron Lyle heavyweight fight in 1976. This fight was strictly a thrilling slugfest between two heavy punchers who took turns putting each other on the canvas until Foreman closed the show with a 5th round knockout win. It was truly an exciting battle with no heavyweight world title at stake.

The fight that probably held the most significance in the 1950's decade was when Rocky Marciano knocked out Joe Walcott in 13 rounds in 1952 to take his world title. This victory would be the beginning of a 4-year reign as heavyweight champion for Marciano which ended when he retired undefeated in 1956.

My choice for the fight of the decade of the 1950's is the 1958 thriller between defending light heavyweight champion Archie Moore versus his challenger: Yvon Durelle of Canada.

Ageless Archie, at 42 years of age, had been the light heavyweight champion since 1952 when he took the title from Joey

159

Maxim in St. Louis. Moore had failed in his 2 attempts to win the heavyweight championship when he was stopped by Rocky Marciano in 1955 and by Floyd Patterson in 1956. Archie rebounded by knocking out Tony Anthony in a 1957 defense of his light heavyweight title in Los Angeles, California.

Durelle was a rugged Canadian who had been boxing professionally since 1949 and had youth in his favor. He was a brutal Canadian slugger with little boxing finesse. Beyond that, he was the current Canadian and British Commonwealth Light Heavyweight champion going into the fight.

The light heavyweight title fight was held on December 10th, 1958 in Montreal, Canada where Durelle was a big fan favorite and had the home crowd advantage. Moore was a heavy favorite going into the title fight, and Durelle was only given a puncher's chance of winning the fight.

Both fighters came out for the fight cautiously and then Durelle exploded with a looping overhand right that came down and caught Moore flush on the side of his jaw. Moore dropped right to the canvas, flat on his back like he had been shot.

The referee was former Heavyweight champion Jack Sharkey, and he bent down low to shout the count into Moore's ear as he lay flat on his back on the canvas. It appeared that Moore would never beat the count until he started to stir at the count of 6. Somehow he managed to roll to his side and then purposefully onto one knee. He stood up just as the referee was shouting 10. Some observers in the crowd felt that Moore was given the benefit of a slow count by Sharkey.

Sharkey ordered the fight to continue. A half-push and half-punch put Moore on the canvas for the second time for a no count by Sharkey. In the final minute of the 1st round, Durelle hit Moore with another monstrous right hand that dropped him to the canvas for the third time in the round. Moore, again, barely beat the count. At the final bell Moore wobbled to his corner on shaky legs.

Durelle attacks Moore in the second round
From: *The Ageless Warrior* by Mike Fitzgerald

Durelle fought cautiously in the 2nd round, as he had punched himself out with his all-out assault in the first round. Moore used the 2nd round to gather his senses and stay away from Durelle's powerful right hand. Durelle picked up the pace in the 3rd round, and he continued the onslaught until he finally dropped Moore to the canvas again in the 5th round with another big right hand to the head. Moore, still again, beat the 10 count just as Durelle appeared to become discouraged. In the 6th round Moore caught his second wind, and he began scoring with combinations. In the 7th round Moore dropped Durelle for the first time in the fight. Durelle returned to his corner at the end of the 7th round tired, as Moore had taken all of his punishment, and he was still, somehow, standing.

Moore took control of the fight in the 8th round and dropped Durelle hard to the canvas near the end of the 10th round. Durelle was all but finished as he came out for the 11th round: throwing wild right hands trying to end the fight immediately. Moore countered Durelle's wild swings and dropped his tired challenger to the canvas for the 10 count in the 11th round to end the most exciting fight of the decade. Several boxing publications made this fight their choice for the Fight of the Decade.

Durelle drives Moore into the ropes in the 10th round
Great Moments in Boxing Winter 1970

Some Canadian writers blamed Referee Sharkey's slow count in the first round for costing Durelle the championship. Some writers pointed out that Sharkey did not begin his count until Durelle was actually in a neutral corner after the first knockdown in the 1st round. The Canadian writers claimed that the referee should have picked up the timekeeper's count as soon as Moore landed on the canvas.

The dramatic finish of a spectacular fight as Moore drives
Durelle to the canvas for the full count in the 11th round
From: *The Ageless Warrior* by Mike Fitzgerald

This fight was Moore's last great performance even though he successfully regained his title several more times before he retired. Moore stopped Durelle in 3 one sided rounds in a rematch in 1959, and he defended his title for the last time against Italian Guilio Rinaldi in 1961 in New York.

This was the most exciting championship fight in the 1950's and, in my opinion, the fight of the decade. Yes, it was even more exciting than Rocky Marciano winning the heavyweight title in 1952, which was a close second for the pure drama of the fight.

DR. RITA BERMUDEZ, MD, MSEE.

Dr. Rita B. Bermudez is a Sacramento, California based Medical Doctor who is Board certified in Sports Medicine, and Pain Management, as well as Physical Medicine and Rehabilitation. Dr. Bermudez also has a Master of Science in Electrical Engineering from Stanford University in California. Dr. Bermudez in the following chapters discusses the topics of Concussions in boxing, and reviews what went wrong in two separate fights which resulted in a fighter's death. Dr. Bermudez reviews the fights between Randie Carver vs. Karbary Salem in 1999, and Max Baer vs. Frankie Campbell in 1930. Dr. Bermudez also talks about how professional boxing could be made into a safer sport.

CHAPTER # 11   CONCUSSIONS AND BOXING

DR. RITA BERMUDEZ, MD, MSEE.

With the death of two boxers within 4 days of each other in 2019, (Maxim Dadashev, and Hugo Alfredo Santillán) there came another outcry to make boxing safe and to prevent brain injury. Blows to the head are more frequent in boxing than any other sport.

A concussion is a disruption of brain activity caused by a blow to the head. It occurs when a strike to the skull causes the brain to bounce back and forth inside the skull, crashing against the hard, bony walls. However, fortunately, the brain floats in a fluid bath that helps to absorb and cushion some of this impact. Still, the act of the brain slamming into the skull can crush, stretch, and damage brain tissue or tear blood vessels. Brain tissue and cells rupture and can release chemicals that temporarily overload the neural circuits of the brain and cause a "time out" reflected as a temporary loss of alertness or other symptoms such as confusion, nausea, sluggishness, or a headache. As more of the brain is traumatized a person may suffer amnesia, blurred vision, inability to focus, or inability to coordinate their movements. If the brain suffers a large shock, then the brain will temporarily fail to respond, and a person will be "knocked out." Using measurements from Frank Bruno, a popular study from 1985 showed that a professional boxer's punch could achieve a blow of about .63 tons to the head which would be the equivalent of an acceleration of 53 times the force of gravity.[1]

A "knockout" is more likely to occur when a larger part of the brain is struck. This is why hitting the jaw is so effective in knocking a person out. A blow to the jaw creates a back and forth bouncing of the brain inside the skull like a whiplash injury. However, a strike to the jaw also causes the head to rotate around the neck and, therefore, the brain also rotates inside the skull shearing along the bony surfaces damaging much more brain tissue. With that much brain trauma, a knockout is very likely. A person who has a longer distance from the jaw to the neck (a long lever arm) can experience a very rapid rotation of the head with a punch and consequently severe twisting and bouncing of the brain inside the skull. This is a recipe for a rapid knock out.

After a concussion, the brain is particularly sensitive to reinjury. This is why doctors recommend avoiding additional head trauma for anywhere from 3 to 120 days after a concussion - *even if* the person seems completely recovered. Current recommendations of the Association of Ringside Physicians can be found online.[2] Repeated concussions increase the risk of cumulative damage to the brain that can lead to chronic traumatic encephalopathy (CTE). This was also known as "punch drunk" syndrome. In a 2019 study, it was estimated that up to 28% of boxers suffer from CTE and there is no cure for the dementia, memory loss, impulsivity, anxiety, depression, or Parkinson's that can be symptoms of this disease.[3] Even more worrisome is that the effects of this damage may not become obvious until years after the brain damage has occurred.

[1] Atha J, Yeadon MR, Sandover J, Parsons KC. The damaging punch. Br Med J (Clin Res Ed). 1985 Dec 21-28;291(6511):1756-7. doi: 10.1136/bmj.291.6511.1756. PMID: 3936571; PMCID: PMC141917

[2] Neidecker J, Sethi NK, Taylor R, et al. Concussion management in combat sports: consensus statement from the Association of Ringside Physicians. *Br J Sports Med.* 2019;53(6):328-333. doi:10.1136/bjsports-2017-098799.

[3] Bieniek, K.F., Blessing, M.M., Heckman, M.G., Diehl, N.N., Serie, A.M., Paolini, M.A., II, Boeve, B.F., Savica, R., Reichard, R.R. and Dickson, D.W. (2020), Association between contact sports participation and chronic traumatic encephalopathy: a retrospective cohort study. Brain Pathol, 30: 63-74. https://doi.org/10.1111/bpa.12757

Risk factors for CTE include boxing for more than a decade, a high number of knockouts, boxing in over 150 bouts, and a person's genetic makeup. People with certain genetic genotypes, (specifically the apolipoprotein E4 phenotype), had a decreased ability to recover from a head injury.[4] Furthermore, a 1997 study showed that boxers with the apolipoprotein E genotype and more than 11 professional bouts, had increased evidence of chronic brain injury.[5]

Dr. Charles Bernick at the Cleveland Clinic has been studying boxers for up to six years to find out more about changes in the brain due to repeated head trauma. His controlled study from 2019, looked at the brain of 240 boxers. Among active fighters, regions of the brain that transmit sensory and motor information and regulate alertness had declined significantly over time. Whereas in the retired fighters, the areas associated with Alzheimer's and CTE, were the brain structures that showed the most decline."[6] Fighters with a significant decline in areas near the center of the brain (the caudate) could not process information as quickly, but otherwise there was no cognitive difference between controls and boxers. However, the caudate is also involved in coordinating muscle movements and is related to Parkinson's disease, attention, and working memory. Still, this study was done over just a few years and the effects of CTE can take decades to develop, so this study needs to be extended for decades to fully assess the effects of repetitive head trauma.

So, what can we do to decrease the risk of head injury besides avoiding head trauma? There is an interesting study on high school football players that states that neck strength decreased the rate of head concussions. For every one-pound increase in neck strength, the

[4] Zazryn TR, McCrory PR, Cameron PA. Neurologic injuries in boxing and other combat sports. Phys Med Rehabil Clin N Am. 2009 Feb;20(1):227-39, x-xi. doi: 10.1016/j.pmr.2008.10.004. PMID: 19084773.

[5] Jordan BD, Relkin NR, Ravdin LD, Jacobs AR, Bennett A, Gandy S. Apolipoprotein E epsilon4 associated with chronic traumatic brain injury in boxing. JAMA. 1997;278(2):136-140. 13. Tierney RT, Mansell JL, Higgins M, et al. Apolipoprotein E

[6] Bernick C, Shan G, Zetterberg H, Banks S, Mishra VR, Bekris L, Leverenz JB, Blennow K. Longitudinal change in regional brain volumes with exposure to repetitive head impact. Neurology Jan 2020, 94 (3) e232-e240; DOI:10.1212/WNL.0000000000008817

odds of a concussion decreased by 5%.[7] The reason is that strong neck muscles help to absorb some of the acceleration of the skull and decrease the amount of force transmitted to the brain. While this study was conducted in football players, it makes sense that it would also apply to boxers. Boxers with strong, short necks like Mike Tyson would expect to be favored in this sense.

Mouth guards work in conjunction with neck strength because one can clench harder using a mouth guard. This clenching of the mouth flexes the neck and brings the chin down. This shortens the lever arm from the chin to the neck and tightens up the neck muscles. For this reason, boxers are often told to keep their chin down. All of this helps to reduce the acceleration of the head caused by a blow.

Consider the subject of sparring. A boxer spends more time sparring than fighting in actual matches, so the effect of sparring on brain trauma needs to be further analyzed. Researchers from the University of Stirling tested 20 amateur boxers after nine minutes of sparring. An hour after sparring, the fighter's performance on memory tests was 52% worse and there was a decrease in motor control and motor coordination.[8] These effects did resolve by 24 hours. However, this does emphasize the need for recovery after blows to the head. Because time for recovery after a concussion is so critical, additional blows to the head should be avoided right after a fight in which a concussion has occurred. This is due to the exquisite sensitivity of the brain to additional trauma as a result of swelling and inflammation as it tries to heal. Therefore, a physician should be consulted about a return to sparring after any concussion of the brain. In addition, a physician should be consulted before allowing a boxing match if the boxer has sustained a concussion prior to the match.

---

[7] C.L. Collins, E.N. Fletcher, S.K. Fields, *et al*. **Neck strength: a protective factor reducing risk for concussion in high school sports** J. Prim. Prev., 35 (5) (2014 Oct), pp. 309-319

[8] Virgilio TG, Letswaart M, Wilon L, Donaldson DI, Hunter AM. Understanding the Consequence of repetitive subconcussive Head Impacts in Sport: Brain Changes and Dampened Motor control are Seen After Boxing Practice. Front. Hum. Neurosci. 2019 Sep. https://doi.org/10.3389/fnhum.2019.00294

Intentional head butts should be disqualifying. Head butts are particularly nasty on several levels. The top of the skull is thick and hard. If a fighter strikes another boxer with the top of his skull, the damage can be tremendous - especially if he hits the side of the head or the chin and causes rotation of the head. In addition, a head butt can easily cut open the skin causing rapid bleeding that, if difficult to control, can stop a fight. This is particularly true if the bleeding obscures vision or is draining into the mouth. The head butt can cause bleeding inside the skull as well. It can have similar effects to being punched with a fist but without the glove. The fighter performing the head butt is not exposed to as much risk because the impact is straight through the skull and in line with the spine, (if done correctly), like thrusting with a spear. So, this prevents the person doing the head butt from getting the rotational movements of the brain which are so much more damaging. However, there is still potential injury for the person performing the head butt. For instance, in studies done on soccer players, who frequently head butt the ball, it is known that repetitive butting of the ball can cause long term brain injury. This might seem like a low force injury but recall that a soccer ball can travel up to 50 mph when a player tries to completely reverse its course by heading the ball. Soccer players who head butted the ball more than 1,550 times a year had signs of brain trauma on MRI scan and they also exhibited impaired memory, attention, and planning.[9,10,11,12] It is reasonable to believe that the same injuries will occur when boxers use head butts. Furthermore, we do have an example of the danger of head butts with the Kabary Salem versus Randie Carver fight. Carver received numerous head butts in earlier rounds of the fight. Carver became increasingly more tired or sluggish as the fight went on which was likely due to

[9] Bailes JE, Petraglia AL, Omalu BI, Nauman E, Talavage T. Role of subconcussion in repetitive mild traumatic brain injury. *J Neurosurg* (2013) 119:1235–45.10.3171/2013.7.JNS121822

[10] Lipton ML, Kim N, Zimmerman ME, Kim M, Stewart WF, Branch CA, et al. Soccer heading is associated with white matter microstructural and cognitive abnormalities. *Radiology* (2013) 268:850–7.10.1148/radiol.13130545

[11] Matser JT, Kessels AG, Jordan BD, Lezak MD, Troost J. Chronic traumatic brain injury in professional soccer players. *Neurology* (1998) 51:791–6.10.1212/WNL.51.3.791

[12] Tysvaer AT, Løchen EA. Soccer injuries to the brain: a neuropsychologic study of former soccer players. *Am J Sports Med* (1991) 19:56–60.10.1177/036354659101900109

bleeding in the brain. He finally collapsed in the 10th round. The neurosurgeon who worked to save him noted that there was significant swelling and bleeding of the brain when he opened the skull to try to relieve the pressure. Unfortunately, Carver did not survive his injuries.

Ringside doctors should be mandatory at boxing events and have the ability to call a timeout if he/she suspects an injury. Some would argue that the doctor should have the ability to call the fight as well. However, the referee is certainly in a better position to observe the fighters and make a quick assessment. If the referee is sufficiently trained, it is reasonable to let a properly trained referee make the call; although I personally think that both the ringside doctor and the referee should be able to end the fight. The boxer's corner, which probably has a more intimate knowledge of the boxer's habits and when he is showing signs of distress, should also have the ability to throw in the towel.

In addition, the weigh-in process needs to be better monitored. Since the fluid bath which the brain is floating in is such an important protective factor, any dehydration before a fight is dangerous. Yet, boxers cut weight rapidly to make their weight class before a fight and this requires dehydration. Dehydration causes headaches, muscle aches, impaired heart performance, and a general decrease in mental clarity which is not good for someone about to be engaged in a sport that taxes all of a combatant's faculties. If a fighter loses 5% of his body weight, his work capacity can decline up to 30%.[13] After cutting, the athlete has just 24 hours to try to rehydrate and this is probably not sufficient time to fully rehydrate the brain.

Clearly there are many issues that need further investigation so that concussions and the long-term consequences of brain trauma in

---

[13] Jeukendrup, Asker, and Michael Gleeson. "Dehydration and Its Effects on Performance." Humankinetics. N.p., n.d. Web. 29 July 2015

boxing can be minimized. No sporting event should end in the death of the athletes involved.

CHAPTER # 12   CAMPBELL VS. BAER

DR. RITA BERMUDEZ, MD, MSEE.

Let's take a look at the factors contributing to a concussion injury using a fight that ended in a tragic fatality. This example is the notorious match between Frankie Campbell and Max Baer. The fight, which occurred in 1930, involved the 6'2½" Max Baer and the 5'10" Frankie Campbell. Baer weighed in at 194 pounds and Campbell at 179. Baer had an amazing arm span which could land a deadly right hand. The Boxing Register: International Boxing Hall of Fame Official Record Book called it "the most powerful right hand in heavyweight history."

Neither fighter seemed to have any underlying medical problems. Campbell had been training for about six months before the fight. Still, Harry Smith of the SF Chronicle commented that Campbell didn't seem to be in top shape, but similar comments had also been made about Baer who rather liked to party and dance with a host of beautiful women rather than train intensely. Before the fight both fighters were told by the State Athletic Commission to "keep fighting as long as the other man is on his feet". Unfortunately, that is exactly what happened.

The fight begins and Campbell follows his planned script of pommeling Baer's trunk. In the second round, Campbell either clipped Baer or Baer slipped, but in any case Baer hit the canvas. Unfazed, Baer bounced back up quickly. Carelessly, Campbell turned his back on Baer as he waved to the crowd. Baer capitalized on the opportunity to come up from behind and gave

Campbell a tremendous right-hand punch to the back of his head. The referee, Toby Irwin, could have disqualified Baer or warned Campbell but did neither. Campbell was dazed but did not fall and seemed to be okay when he came out for the third round but had commented that he felt "something snap in his head."

Campbell again fought well for the next two rounds until the fatal fifth. At that point, Baer hurt Campbell with a tremendous left hook to the jaw which drove him into the ropes. Baer followed Campbell into the corner and hurt him again with a right cross sending him trapped in the corner against the ring post. Campbell's hands were down, and he was not fighting back. Campbell was totally out of it and he could not fall because he was entangled in the ropes. Campbell could no longer protect himself, but Baer kept slugging away at Campbell's head – which repeatedly smashed into the large metal turnbuckle holding the ropes. This was so bad, the back of Campbell's head (and his face) were a bloody pulp. Campbell could not fall down as the momentum of the repeated punches kept him up against the ropes. When the referee Irwin finally intervened, Campbell slumped to the floor and was motionless. There was no ring side doctor but two doctors in the audience did work their way through the crowd and try to revive Campbell to no avail. They stated that Campbell was hemorrhaging from his eyes and nose. The ambulance arrived approximately 30 minutes later to take him to the hospital where Campbell died the next morning.

This fight emphasizes several interventions that could have made a difference. First a great deal has been said about the punch Baer gave Campbell from behind and the report that Campbell felt something snap in his head. However, the fact that Campbell went on to fight two good rounds without any signs of increasing impairment suggests that this was *not* the catastrophic injury. Furthermore, there is no reference to any fractures in Campbell's autopsy. In fact, the autopsy states that Campbell had double hemorrhages - essentially bleeding from both sides of the head. In reality, he had *multiple* hemorrhages. Still, being hit from behind without any chance to defend one's self is inherently dangerous, and Baer should have been stopped from delivering the blow by putting him through a count before resumption of the fight or otherwise warning Campbell.

Campbell not only suffered massive intracranial bleeding, but he also lost the connective tissue mooring between the brain and the skull such that his brain was just a free-floating mass. While the brain does float in a fluid bath, there is an arachnoid membrane that is made up of multiple stretchy filaments that help to support and suspend the brain in this fluid bath, and this is further re-enforced by a tougher outer membrane. Think of the arachnoid membrane like a spider web that helps to keep the brain roughly attached to the skull but allows some movement - like a stretchy net. The combination of the fluid bath and the membrane dampens movements of the brain and helps protect it from blows. In addition, there are multiple blood vessels that travel within these membranes and when the brain is hit, these vessels can tear bleeding into the spaces between the membrane, the brain, and the skull. The autopsy report stated Campbell's brain was completely detached from any connective tissue support. Clearly, this kind of damage could not happen with one blow. Instead, this damage would have to be from the repeated blows to the skull basically ricocheting the brain back and forth and rupturing blood vessels and tearing the supporting membranes. Bleeding in the brain further pulled the brain from its supporting membranes – peeling the two apart. This caused further damage by cutting off oxygen supply and increasing the pressure on the brain tissues which were pressed against the bony skull. Add to this the amplification of the blow by the head bouncing off of the metal turnbuckle which caused a rebound blow on the back side of Campbell's head. Therefore, it is no wonder that Campbell's brain was bleeding practically everywhere. It seems unlikely that Campbell would have survived *unaffected* from this beating, but perhaps if there had been a ringside doctor and an ambulance on site – he might have, at least, survived. It would have required emergent surgery to release the pressure from bleeding on the brain. However, doctors later said that this surgery was too late to help by the time Campbell reached the hospital. Brain specialist Tilton E. Tillman "declared death had been caused by a succession of blows on the jaw and not by any strike on the rear of the head. Campbell's brain was knocked completely loose from his skull. If it had been a case of one cerebral hemorrhage, or two, or even three, we might have saved his life. But his brain tissue literally was one huge mass of bruises. There was nothing to be done."

So, one critical issue here was to stop the fight as soon as Campbell was clearly dazed and no longer defending himself. This should have been done by the referee or by Campbell's corner throwing in the towel. It is not clear if Campbell's corner had a clear view of the fight, but one would think the referee did have such a view. Campbell's corner reportedly did, although Toby Irwin later said he was behind Baer without a clear view. As far as Campbell's corner, Cal Working, who could see his fighter was dazed, said he had screamed to stop the fight, but Toby Irwin said he did not hear him. If there had been a ringside doctor, circumstances might have been drastically different, especially if the doctor had the ability to call a time out. This fight makes it clear that there needs to be a ringside doctor. In fact, where life or death is concerned, it makes sense to have more than one set of eyes calling a fight. It is for this reason, I would advocate that the referee, the doctor, and the corner all having the ability to call the fight and/or at least call a time out. Furthermore, all parties should be trained on when to intervene and to intervene earlier rather than later.

The other factor was the ring design at the time, which left the dangerous turnbuckle exposed as a weapon against the fighter. The fact that the ring was designed so that the ropes attached directly to the ring post allowed Campbell's head to be stuck against the turnbuckle. Fortunately, ring design has improved since the 30's.

The other consideration this fight underscores is the advantage of standing 8 counts. This would have given the referee and the corner crucial time in which to better assess Campbell's status.

While this fight focuses on preventing acute death due to concussion, we also need to be just as concerned about the long-term effects of concussion injuries and how these can be prevented from causing long-term sequelae to those who are engaging in the sport. Therefore, it is important to keep analyzing the causes and consequences of injuries and updating the sport to try to make it as safe as possible.

Bibliography

Information from the following publications was used in preparation for this book.

The Ring Magazine, August 1950

Boxing and Wrestling, March 1953

Boxing Yearbook 1954 Edition

Television Boxing Guide 1954, Windsor Press

The Ring Magazine, May 1955

The Ring Magazine, June 1955

The Ring Magazine, April 1956

Boxing and Wrestling, November 1958

Boxing and Wrestling, January 1960

Victory over Myself, Floyd Patterson 1963

Boxing Illustrated, August 1970

Great Moments in Boxing, Winter 1970

Sugar Ray, Sugar Ray Robinson, 1971

Boxing Illustrated, October 1973

Rocky Marciano Biography of a First Son, Everett M. Skeehan, 1977

The Ring Record Book, 1980

The Ring Record Book, 1981

*The Encyclopedia of Boxing, Gilbert Odd,*1989

Boxing Updates, Flash, September, 1999

Rocky Marciano The Rock of his Times, Russell Sullivan.2002

The Ageless Warrior by Mike Fitzgerald 2004

Box Rec.com

Acknowledgements

This book would not have been possible without the help and guidance of the following people.

Aaron Lingenfelter, Chief Editor

Dr. Rita B. Bermudez, Medical research

Robert Johr, Cover design and support

Lt. David P. Brida, Historical research, CDC

About the Author

The author, Larry Carli, is a retired Sheriff Detective and District Attorney Criminal Investigator from Sacramento County, California. He has published three books titled *The Illinois Thunderbolt*, the life story of boxer Billy Papke, and *The Top Ten Middleweight Champions of All Time* and *Boxing's Super 70s*. He has also written freelance boxing stories for *International Boxing Research Organization*, *Boxing Illustrated*, *Fight Beat*, and *The Ring Magazine*.

The author is also a former member of the International Boxing Research Organization, the National Sportscasters and Sportswriters Association, and the California Writers Club.

www.ingramcontent.com/pod-product-compliance
Lightning Source LLC
Chambersburg PA
CBHW071435090426
42737CB00011B/1670